CHINESE BRAID EMBROIDERY

By
Jacqui Carey

Fig. 2.
A Bai collar with several different braids bordering the embroidered fabric shapes.
Courtesy of Martin Conlan.

Published by Carey Company, Ottery St Mary, Devon, UK.
The author and agents of this publication can accept no responsibility for any consequential loss or damage to person or property arising from the content of any part of this publication.

Copyright © 2007 Jacqui Carey

All rights reserved
No part of this publication may be reproduced, stored in a retrieval system, or transmitted in any other form or by any means, electronic, mechanical, photo-copying, recording or otherwise, without prior permission of the Publisher.
Printed by Mccgraphic-Elkar, Spain.

ISBN 0 9523225 6 0

Acknowledgements

I first became aware of Chinese braid embroidery at an exhibition at West Surrey College of Art & Design, Farnham in 1994. The display of Miao costume from Gina Corrigan's collection was accompanied by a book written by Deryn O'Connor. Anyone with an interest in textiles would not fail to be overwhelmed by the shear quantity and quality of textile skills found in these costumes. Although the braid work is just a small aspect of the costume, it soon became apparent that there was more to it than first met the eye, and so the journey began. Gina Corrigan's assistance has been fundamental to this project, from her generosity in allowing me access to her collection, to the sharing of her knowledge. She also organised a tailor-made trip to China to meet and interview braidmakers in Guizhou, a trip that added the 'human' factor to the many braids studied. My thanks also goes to our fellow travellers, Ruth Smith, Helen Wolfe and Shelagh Fitzgibbon, and our interpreter Wang Jun. I would also like to thank Diane Gaffney, who's enthusiasm and expertise was so valued in our subsequent travelling.

I have had the privilege of being able to study many private and public collections. I would like to thank everyone who kindly allowed me access to their treasures, and for the permission to publish photographs which are acknowledged individually (unacknowledged images are from the author's own collection). Particular mention should go to Martin Conlan (of Slow Loris) and Ien Rappoldt, who not only allowed me access to a wealth of material, but also shared their intimate knowledge of years of travelling in China. Thanks also to the assistance provided by Helen Wolfe at the British Museum, Ailsa Laxton at the Museum of East Asian Art, Helen Persson at the Victoria & Albert Museum, Frances Pritchard at the Whitworth Art Gallery, as well as many other museum and library staff.

A research project, such as this, is a combined effort, with help and leads coming from many quarters. Assistance has been provided by so many, that a list would be seemingly endless. However, I would like to make particular mention of the following people: Ji Zhou Zhen, Li Fung, Li Jinying, Li Zheng, Lisheng Ying, Liu Yao Yang, Liu Zong Yan, Lizhing Hua, Pang Sheng Feng, Pan Sheng Zhen, Wang Enying, Wuxiu Zhen, Xiong Guiyang, Mrs Yang, Meg Andrews, Nancy Berliner, Eric Boudet, Gil Dye, Beverley Jackson, Paul Prentice, Glenn Roberts and Jacqueline Simcox. My thanks also goes to Anne Dyer, Jan Rawdon-Smith and Ien Rappoldt who's encouragement prompted me to continue with this particular folly, as well as Veronica Johnston and Sonia Jupp, who also added their expertise in proof reading. As always, I am grateful for my family's continued forbearance, and for their assistance in helping me turn this information into a book, especially Richard Carey for his graphics work.

But most of all, I am deeply indebted to all the Chinese women who so generously shared their skills with me, both directly and indirectly. Without their expertise there would not have been a book to write.

Fig. 1 (front and inside cover).
Detail from an old Miao panel. It is covered in dense braid embroidery, giving it a rich sculpted appearance. Different braid structures and patterns have been applied using various methods. The main body of the dragon motif is built up from overlaid loops, with a border of pleating and rounded zigzag spines.
Courtesy of Gina Corrigan.

Map of China

Fig. 3.
Map of China and its provinces.

Contents

Acknowledgements 3
Contents 5
Introduction 6
Evolution & Change
    Early Evidence 7
    Shoes 12
    Methods 16
    Chinese Development or
        Foreign Import 18
    The Miao 26
    Today & Tomorrow 30
Materials & Equipment
    Braiding Threads 34
    Braiding Stands 36
    Braiding Bobbins 44
    Paper Templates 54
    Fabric 56
    Needles & Thread 57
Braiding
    Introduction 58
    Reading the Instructions 60
    Adding More Thread 60
    Getting Started 61
    Braid JC1 63
    Braid JC2 66
    Braid JC3 67
    Braid JC4 68
    Braid JC5 70
    Braid JC6 72
    Braid JC7 76
    Braid JC8 77
    Braid JC9 78
    Braid JC10 85
    Braid JC11 88
    Braid JC12 90
    Braid JC13 92
    Braid JC14 95
    Braid JC15 98
    Braid JC16 99
    Braid JC17 100

Embroidery
    Introduction 103
    Flat Straight Border 105
    Curves & Corners
        Eased 106
        Puckered 106
        Tucked 106
        Coiled 106
        Folded 106
    Regular Repeats
        'Figure-of-Eight' Design ... 110
        'Fret' Design 111
        'Looped Border' Design .. 112
        'Scalloped' Design 113
        'Rounded Zigzag' Design.. 114
        'Angular Zigzag' Design... 115
    Motifs
        Outlines 116
        Flat Fillings 117
        Pleating 118
        Coiling 120
        Triangular Coiling 122
        Overlaid Loops 124
Notes 126
Bibliography 127

Introduction

Tradition is not static, but a gradual process of loss and gain, with threads of continuity that connect together a sense of the same.

Braid embroidery[1] (chan xiu) is just one of the many wonderful textile traditions found in China. This book is intended as a 'snapshot' of the technique taken at this point in time, with a brief prelude to place it in a wider history. It aims to record some of the practical knowledge that is traditionally passed down by verbal and visual means. It is a knowledge that is increasingly being ignored in today's desire for speedier alternatives. The book is also an attempt to recover some of the skills of the anonymous makers, whose unwritten testimony is preserved in their work. As with any 'snapshot', it will always be a partial view, a single picture taken from one perspective, of an ever changing and wide-ranging situation.

There are many forms of braiding, both in style and technique. Although various types have been found in China, this book concentrates on a variety of stand and bobbin braiding. It is a technique that is still practised today in southwest China. The resulting braids are of a distinctive style. They are flat and narrow, typically between 1 and 5 mm^2 in width. There are also certain characteristics found in their structure.[3] They are usually made from silk and are used for decorative work, being couched down onto costume and accessories.

As with many traditional textiles, this form of braid embroidery work is in decline. It is a time consuming activity, and the fine detail of the finished work is increasingly being overlooked and undervalued. As a consequence, fewer people are learning, or

Fig. 4.
Shidong Miao girl wearing traditional costume whilst staying in touch with the modern world.
Courtesy of Ien Rappoldt.

Introduction

using, the skill. Although the interest in this craft is decreasing, it is unlikely to die out completely. At present, braid appliqué is best known as a Miao[4] craft, and a speciality of Guizhou Province. The Miao are renowned for their costume and their textile skills. These attributes have been highlighted as an attraction for the expanding tourist market, which caters for both Chinese and overseas visitors. No doubt this will provide the incentive to preserve certain aspects of textile skill. It appears that the loss will be in the rich variety that has existed. To date, well over 100 different variations of braid structure have been analysed. These have been found on Chinese textiles held in collections here in the West. Yet observation of existing practice in China has revealed only a handful.[5] It is hoped that this book will preserve some elements of the technique, opening them up for a wider audience to understand and appreciate.

Note on terminology.

The contemporary practitioners in China do not have a standard terminology for this technique. This presents problems when writing about the subject, especially when it is compounded with translation issues. Makers often refer to their work in broad terms, without feeling the need to be more precise about their equipment, methods or results. However, in order to distinguish between the finer details included in this book, a more Western approach has been taken. Consequently, the technical terms used in this book are of the author's own choosing. Note also that when references have been made to individual braidmakers, their names are given in the eastern form, with the surname followed by given name. Apologies must be made for any errors that might have arisen during the process of translation.

Fig. 5.
Skills are handed down from the older generation. Here, Lisheng Ying helps 24 year-old Liu Yao Yang with her braid embroidery. Taijiang County, Guizhou.

Evolution & Change

Early Evidence.

Although braid embroidery is still practised in China, little is known about its origin. China has long held a reputation for producing beautiful and complex textiles, and it is famed as the 'land of silk'. So it is not surprising to find that sophisticated examples of braiding have been unearthed in Chinese excavations.[6] However, these early braids are stylistically different from the narrow silk braids used for the applied work discussed in this book.

These decorative narrow braids start to appear in abundance on items dating from the second half of the 19th century. Only a few earlier examples have been found. But as there is a scarcity of textile material from earlier periods, and an uncertainty in some dating, it is difficult to determine the exact starting point of this style of work. What is of interest, is the widespread nature of the braid embroidery. Although examples have been found throughout China, there is a higher frequency on items from the south-east.[7] The braid embroidery often forms a highlight to the border edge of a garment or accessory. This manner of work can be found on a wide range of items, such as robes, skirts, collars, hats, shoes, cushions,

Evolution & Change

Fig. 6.
This Han Chinese lady's silk robe was collected in 1907 (detail on left). It shows the typical use of braid. The tiny braid is couched down as a highlight to the border decoration, and is used in conjunction with woven silk ribbon and stitch embroidery. The braid's red background with a white spot, was, and still is, a popular pattern. It can be found on many different braid structures. This version is similar in construction to braid JC6 (page 72).
Courtesy of the Cadbury family collection.

Evolution & Change

purses, and auspicious artefacts. In most early examples, the braids are laid flat as an outline border, either straight, or following the contours of the edge. In these instances, they are used in addition to other decorative features, such as woven ribbons and stitch embroidery. Indeed, the braids are often overlooked, not just because of their tiny nature, but by the fact that other eye-catching textiles surround them. However, there are some examples where the braid is not used as an edging. Here, the braids curve and coil to form motifs depicting floral, fauna and symbolic patterns.

Fig. 8 (above).
Fine braids, made from metallic threads, were also very popular, especially on Manchu garments. This detail shows a braid following the contours of the decorative border on a late 19th century, 'horseshoe' cuff from a man's jacket. The 8-bobbin, 4-ridge structure is typical of metallic braid.
Courtesy of Meg Andrews.

Fig. 7 (below).
Braids were also applied as decorative motifs. This detail, found on some old trousers, shows different coloured braids forming the outline to a floral motif. It is unusual to see such a loose-tensioned braid with spaces between the threads.

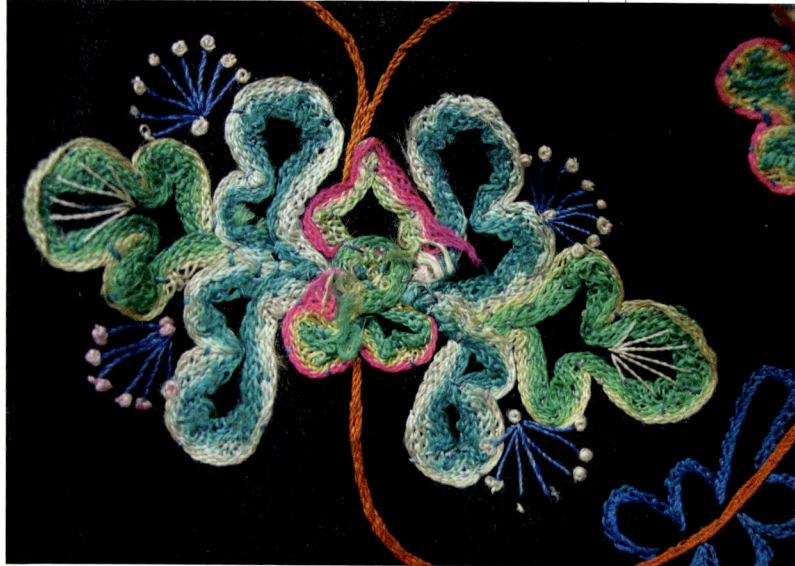

Fig. 9 (opposite page).
A child's collar from the late 19th century. The embroidered silk panels are bordered with a selection of silk braids. They comprise ten different structures, and between eight and sixteen bobbins were used in their production.

Evolution & Change

Evolution & Change

Shoes.

A particularly rich source of examples can be found on the little lotus shoes made for bound feet. Here, the petite nature of the braid is in keeping with the dainty scale of the textile shoe. Although these particular shoes are often considered grotesque in today's society, there is a growing understanding of their true position within the Chinese culture (Ko 2001). Here, they were held in high esteem and carried with them a potent symbolic value. Shoemaking was an important part of a woman's life - an opportunity to display one's ability and worth, as well as a means of personal expression. Women, from all classes and regions, devoted much time and attention to the making of shoes. In fact, the importance of shoemaking can still be seen today, as modern shoes are still handmade and worn in many areas.

There is plenty of evidence of women handmaking the entire lotus shoe, as well as working the embroidered decoration. However, it is unclear whether they actually made the braids that they used as ornate borders. Mention has been made of braid pedlars (Jackson 1997:56) who travelled around selling their wares, transporting their goods in large

Fig. 10 (above) & Fig. 11 (opposite page)
Braids often feature on Chinese shoes. The dainty scale of the silk braid is particularly suited to these tiny Lotus shoes made for bound feet. Braid embroidery is often found on shoes originating from the south and east of China. Above: a pair of shoes, showing the detailed work on the sole. Shandong Province. Opposite: A pair of shoes from Shanxi Province.
Courtesy of Paul Prentice

Evolution & Change

— 13 —

Evolution & Change

boxes carried on their backs. The availability of ready-made braid for sale is supported by items held at the British Museum.[8] A selection of handmade braids and woven ribbons was donated to the museum in the late 19th century. They were accompanied by information stating that they originated from Chendu, in Sichuan province, and that this type of work was a speciality of the city. The note went on to say that although women used these items, they were made by men, who sold them from between a halfpenny to one penny per foot length.

The samples are typical of the type of trimmings applied onto items from this era. However, the widespread existence of so many examples, and the variations in their structure, suggests that Chendu was not the only centre of production. Additional written evidence supports the existence of braid and ribbon manufacture in other areas, though the exact nature of the products is debatable (Wilson 1986:62). Comparisons with other textile techniques would suggest that production was not restricted to specific areas, or to modes of output. It is probable that there was a range of different systems, from professionally-made braids intended for the commercial market, to home production for own use.

Today, there remains a tentative connection between the braiding technique and its association with the lotus shoes. Old braiding stands, often made from beautifully carved wood, are sold to the more lucrative market as 'foot binding stools', although there appears to be no evidence to support that they were actually used for this purpose.

Evolution & Change

Fig. 12 (opposite page).
Shoes from Hebei Province.

Fig. 13 (above).
Shoes from Anhui Province. The detail shows several different braids applied as borders and motifs.
Courtesy of Paul Prentice

Evolution & Change

Methods.

While early documents detail various aspects of textile techniques, to date, no mention has been found of the braid work. There are prints and paintings showing activities such as spinning, dyeing, weaving and embroidery, but none that illustrate braiding. There is also a lack of written information about the technique. This is not unusual. Braiding can be found all over the world, but documentation of the subject remains sparse. So, although there are plenty of actual historical examples, as yet, there are no sources of information explaining the exact methods used to produce them.

The stand & bobbin method of braiding shown in this book is based on procedures employed today. But there is another method that should be considered. Loop-manipulation

Fig. 14.
Loop-manipulation is an old and widespread technique. There are different methods of making braids using this technique. Here, the Lao Mien lady on the right holds loops of thread in her fingers. She manoeuvres them through one another to interlace the threads together. The lady on the left tightens the stitches of the finished braid, which is rolled around her waist band.

Evolution & Change

is a way of making braids that is both ancient and far reaching. There have been reports of its use in contemporary China, but these appear to be relatively infrequent.[9] No equipment is required for this technique as loops of thread are held taut in the workers' hands, whilst the other ends are secured in some manner. The loops are then interworked to create the braid.

Goldman (1995:6) states that the Lao Mien[10] use loop-manipulation for making short lengths, and stand & bobbin equipment for longer lengths. This is a practical approach as loop-manipulation is an efficient way of fabricating small quantities. Another braidmaker[11] offered an alternative reason for using both techniques. Although the loop-manipulation method is efficient, it usually requires two people (one to manoeuvre the loops and another to hold, and tension, the growing braid). Whilst the stand & bobbin method is slower, it can be made alone, by just one worker. Lao Mien work illustrates that the same braidmaker can produce exactly the same structured braid by working either of the two methods. Consequently, caution has to be taken when analysing a finished braid. Although one can be certain about the braid's structure, its method of pro-

duction is debatable. However, it is important to realise that the loop-manipulation technique produces braids that have certain structural characteristics. Analysis of the Chinese braids revealed that whilst some of the samples possessed these characteristics, and could have easily been made by either method, there were many others that did not.[12]

As loop-manipulation is rarely known, or used, in China today, it seems likely that the stand & bobbin equipment has gradually superseded the loop-manipulation technique. This scenario can be found elsewhere in the world, for example in Japan. Here, kute-uchi, a handheld loop-manipulation technique, declined at the end of the 19th century, in favour of various different types of stand and bobbin equipment (Kinoshita 1994:336).

Fig. 15.
When analysing an old braid, one can be certain of its structure, but its method of production is debatable. Was this old braid made using the stand & bobbin technique, or loop-manipulation, or by some other means?

Evolution & Change

Chinese Development or Foreign Import?

The lack of evidence means that it is hard to establish whether the stand & bobbin braiding originated in China, or whether it was a foreign import. Certainly there are connections and comparisons that can be made throughout Europe and Asia, but it remains a mystery as to who was influencing whom. Over the centuries there has been trade from east to west, and vice versa. From the earliest chain of exchanges, there arose a flow of ideas and exotic goods. Land routes, such as the silk roads across the top of China to the West, were well established by the 1st century AD. Other, less known, routes to the South and North were also operating from an early age. These land routes were augmented by sea traffic. Arabian, and later Chinese, traders dominated the waters between the Indian and Pacific Oceans. The prolific maritime activity between the two regions provided a major source of cultural exchange. Transportation by sea expanded in the 16th century with the arrival of European fleets. The introduction of direct links between Europe and China increased the availability, and the influence, of foreign culture (Jackson & Jaffer 2004). But, in spite of long-term and widespread trade, the flow of goods and knowledge has never been even, or continual. Issues such as politics, warfare, commerce and fashion have affected the accessibility and exchange of goods and ideas. However, what is certain, is that Chinese braiding did not develop in isolation.

Visually, one of the closest comparisons can be found in early English pattern books. These hand-written books, dating from the 15th to 17th centuries, contain instructions for making loop-manipulated braids. They are often accompanied by an example stitched down onto the page. Many of these fine braids are 3-dimensional, but some of the flat ones are identical, in both structure and visual style, to those found on Chinese items. However, the English braids were intended for the making of purse drawstrings, rather than for use as applied decoration. Nevertheless, the use of braid embroidery to decorate textiles is a common theme all over Europe and Asia, and many examples can be found. Woven ribbons have also been used in the same manner. Although the ribbons can be stitched down in textural and 3-dimensional designs, the visual appearance is different. This is due to the unique nature of a braid structure, compared to that of a woven ribbon. Braids can flex and bend in a distinct way, making them ideally suited to this form of ornamentation.

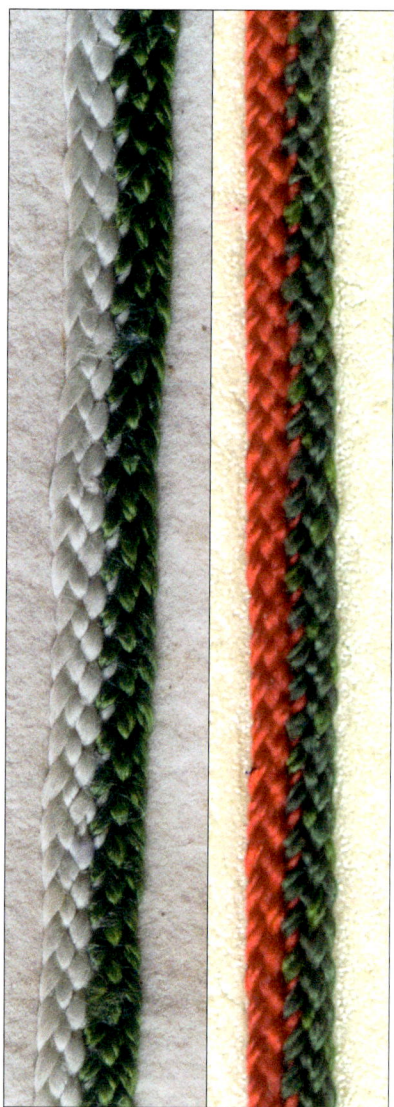

Fig. 16.
The sample on the left has been sewn into a 17th century English book. It accompanies instructions for making loop-manipulated purse strings. The braid sample is identical in structure to the contemporary Chinese one shown on the right. Both samples are made from handspun, 2-ply silk and are less than 4 mm in width.
Courtesy of Wigan Archives Service.

Evolution & Change

LADY'S ALBUM

OF

FANCY WORK

FOR

1850,

CONSISTING OF

NOVEL, ELEGANT, AND USEFUL DESIGNS

IN

𝕶nitting, 𝕹etting, 𝕮rochet, 𝕭raiding, and 𝕰mbroidery,

WITH CLEAR AND EXPLICIT

DIRECTIONS FOR WORKING THE PATTERNS.

PUBLISHED BY
CORNER OF

Fig. 17.
Braid embroidery was fashionable in England during the Victorian era. Pattern books, such as this 'Lady's Album' from 1850, were widely available, and included instructions for decorating items with applied braid. This gentleman's velvet hat is a typical result, and is trimmed with a fine three-coloured, silk braid.
Courtesy of Leicester City Museum Services.

Evolution & Change

European lacemaking is another source of comparison. Here, connections can be made with both the equipment and the method of production. Stand & bobbin lacemaking developed in Europe during the 16th century. Its early progression is shrouded in ambiguity, but it appears to have gradually evolved from earlier passementerie techniques (Levey 1983:5). At its onset, the technique of lacemaking was closely linked with braidmaking, with interaction and exchange between the two techniques. For example, braiding methods were producing 'lace' structures,[13] and lacemaking equipment was being used to produce 'braid' structures.[14] However, as the lacemaking technique flourished, it expanded and diversified, distancing itself from braiding.[15] Different areas throughout Europe started to develop their own distinctive style of lace, with regional variations in methods and equipment.

Although there is no tradition of using, or making, lace in China, it was evidently made there. For example, a late 19th century photograph of a Chinese lacemaker can be seen in Smith's book "Chinese Characteristics". The technique was probably introduced by some of the many missionaries who lived and worked in China, notably during the 19th century.[16] Many European religious institutions were keen advocates of lacemaking, deeming it an appropriate activity for girls in their care. They also played an active role in the education and employment of lacemakers.[17] Although there are many differences

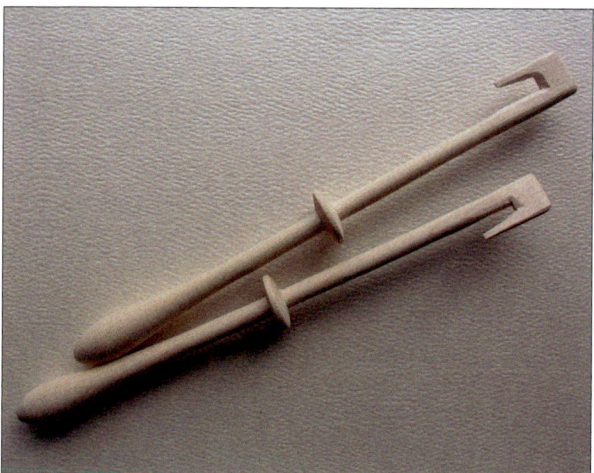

Fig.18.
A pair of lacemaking bobbins from Arbenberg, in Germany. These hook-ended bobbins are used for making lace with metallic threads. They compare well with the hook-shaped bobbins seen in Fig. 59.
Courtesy of Sue Goodman.

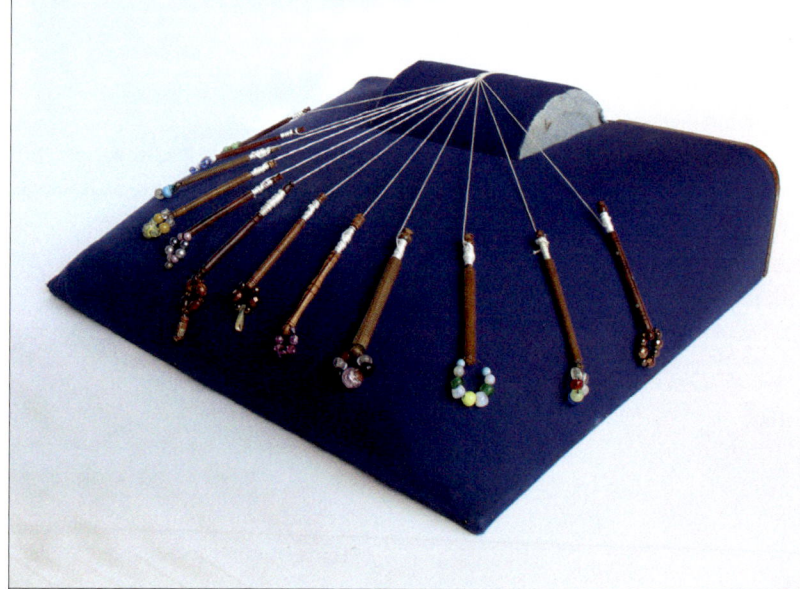

Fig. 19.
Equipment for making European bobbin lace. The threads are wound onto bobbins that rest on the padded working surface. The bobbins are weighted with beads to provide tension for the threads. The bobbins are manipulated to interlace the threads together, and the finished product is gradually wound onto the cylindrical roller. It functions much like the Chinese equipment shown in the next chapter.

Evolution & Change

between modern lacemaking and the technique described in this book, there are also connections. The basic principle of the lace equipment shown in Fig. 19 is the same as the Miao stand in Fig. 41. Both use a roller for winding on the finished product. Both have the working threads coming down from the roller onto the bobbins, which are supported over the stand. The Miao bobbins compare well with English lace bobbins which are 'spangled' (having beads and other assorted objects attached to the end). These weight the bobbins providing a tension on the threads. In addition, the hook-shaped heads of the Chinese bobbins bear a strong resemblance to the European bobbins used for making metallic lace.[18] Hook ended bobbins of this type have also been used in Siberia for making simple braids (Popov 1955:69). There are also similarities in the method of working, as bobbins are lifted in pairs, and taken under and over other bobbins to interlace the threads. The major difference in the style of moves is that, for lacemaking a pair of bobbins are worked together from one edge to the other, whilst the braiding utilises opposite bobbins and works them in mirror image movements from the edge towards the centre.

Other connections can be made with braiding techniques, such as 'Tili,' which is found in the Middle East, and out to the Maldives. This braiding technique is even more reminiscent of lacemaking as the equipment closely resembles the European bolster cushions. The method of construction also mimics the lace technique. The bobbins are manipulated in pairs making a classic lacemaking stitch as they work from edge to edge. The resultant braids, which incorporate thin metallic strips, are used to embellish the traditional costume. The braids are couched down, either flat, or 3-dimensionally, to form decorative designs onto a whole range of garments. Direct comparisons can be made with this style of braid embroidery and the Chinese version shown in this book.

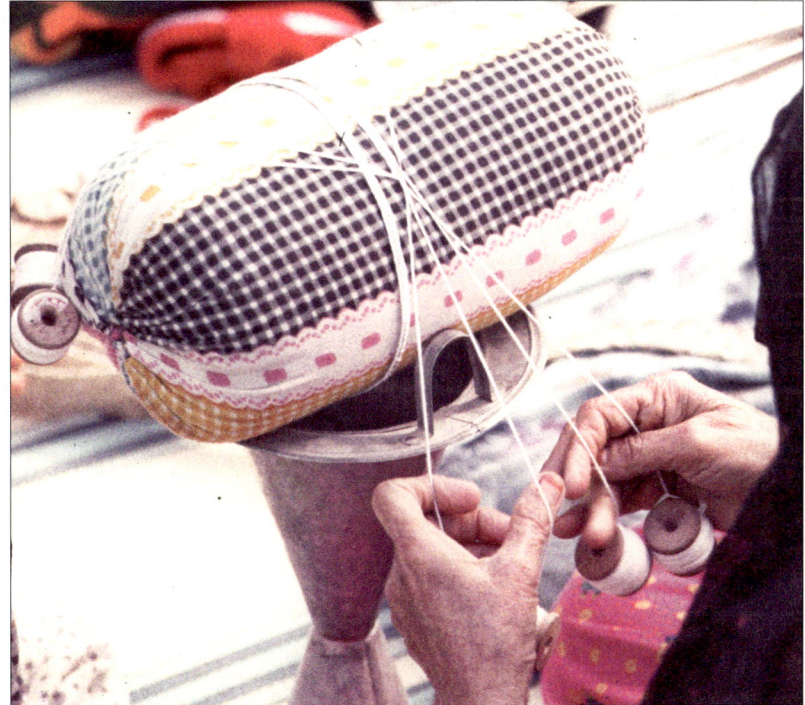

Fig. 20.
A braidmaker from Oman making 'tili'. She works on a padded bolster pillow supported on a metal stand. This is similar to European lacemaking equipment. The threads, wound onto bobbins, are manipulated to produce the braid. The pillow is gradually rotated as work progresses, serving the same purpose as a roller.
Courtesy of Gigi Crocker Jones.

Evolution & Change

Fig. 21.
In the Middle East, braids are couched down in flat and 3-dimensional shapes to form the decoration on traditional costume. This detail, from a Yemeni dress, shows braid embroidery made using the same technique as shown on page 115.
Courtesy of Jenny Balfour-Paul.

Evolution & Change

There is a strong tradition of braidmaking to the east of China, in Japan. It is thought that the technique of loop-manipulation was introduced from China, and stunning examples can be found in the Shosoin repository, dating from the 8th century (Kinoshita 1994). However, these braids were not used for decorative embroidery. Indeed the fashion for using braids in this manner seems to have by-passed Japan. Instead, the Japanese developed the technique and used it extensively for lacing their Samurai armour. By the 20th century, various types of stand & bobbin braiding had superseded loop-manipulated braiding. The origins of the equipment is unclear, though it is thought to have appeared some time during the Edo period (1603-1868 AD). Of the many pieces of equipment that are still in use, none resemble the Chinese stands. The takadai (see Fig. 22) is the closest, with its 'tori' (two uprights and a cross bar) which is shaped like a few of the Miao roller systems (for example see Fig. 47). But, the 'tori' is not a roller system; it is simply a support for the braid as it continues downward to a roller situated below. The Japanese threads are tensioned onto bobbins, but unlike the Chinese ones, these are dumb-bell shaped with internal weights. Although the braid is constructed with threads that start from the outer edges and travel toward the centre, the movements differ in that it is not the bobbins that are handled. Instead a space is opened up between the threads, forming a 'shed,'[19] through which one bobbin is taken. This action has a closer resonance to weaving.

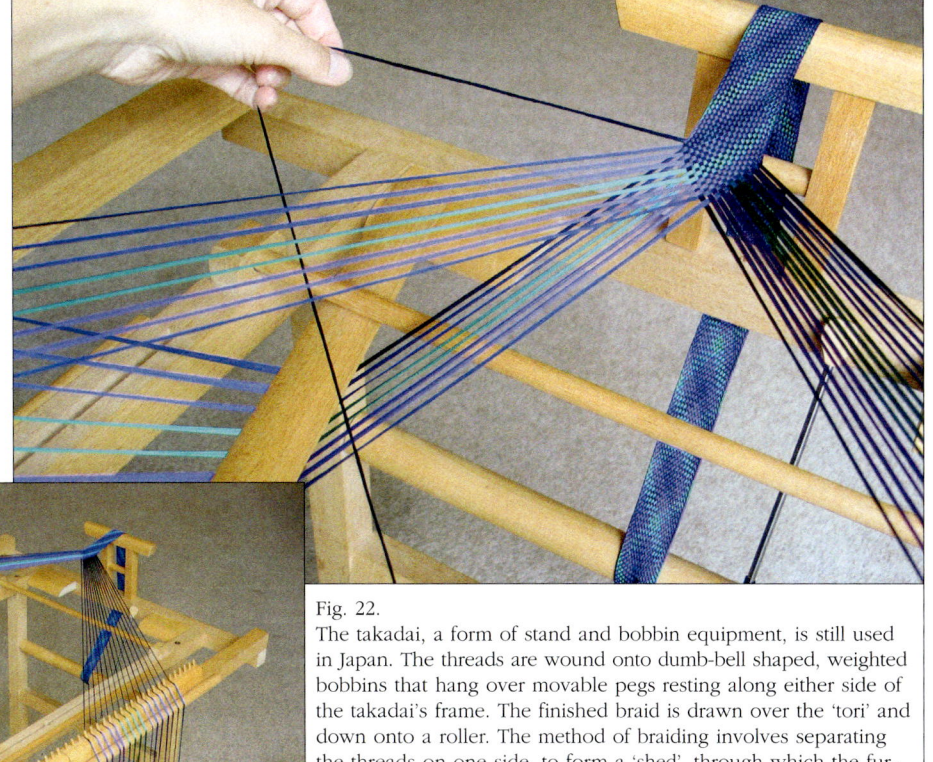

Fig. 22.
The takadai, a form of stand and bobbin equipment, is still used in Japan. The threads are wound onto dumb-bell shaped, weighted bobbins that hang over movable pegs resting along either side of the takadai's frame. The finished braid is drawn over the 'tori' and down onto a roller. The method of braiding involves separating the threads on one side, to form a 'shed', through which the furthest bobbin is passed. This action is similar to weaving.

Evolution & Change

Not surprisingly, the closest comparisons to Chinese braid embroidery are found in the countries that border China. There have been reports of a technique, found in the Gobi regions of Mongolia, which is similar to the stand & bobbin braiding described in this book (Chabros & Batculuun 1993). The technique appears to have been well-known amongst the Khalkha herdsmen at the end of the 19th century, although it has all but died out today.

The description of the equipment, known as 'zoos siree' (which translates as coin-table), is remarkably similar to the equipment that is still used in southern China today (for example see Fig. 50). The flat, circular working surface of the table is approximately 60 to 70 cm in diameter, with a roller system rising up from the rear of the stand. This consists of a rotating roller bar supported within a framework, and jammed with a peg inserted into a hole in the roller bar. Some stands are decorated with carvings, or painted with ornamental designs. A few are collapsible to aid transportation, and some incorporate storage boxes. The threads to be braided are attached onto the roller bar and wound onto the bobbins, which are arranged around the circumference of the stand (see Fig. 25). The Mongolian bobbins are the hook-ended type like the Dong[20] ones seen in Fig. 61. They are weighted with old Chinese coins attached to the bobbins with strips of leather or fabric.

The braids are made either from imported Chinese silk, or from finely spun sheep wool and camel hair. A popular braid is a spot design made from six strands of camel hair and a single strand of white wool. This is similar to the braid shown on page 72. The flat braids were couched down to form decorative borders on garments and accessories, and there appears to have been

Fig. 23.
Ny Ting, a Lao Mien braidmaker, using traditional equipment. The working surface is a basket, covered in an old sarong. She manipulates the weighted bobbins to produce a braid. There is no roller system; the threads and finished braid are simply attached to a stick at the top of the basket.

Evolution & Change

prestige attached to the ability to produce exceptionally narrow braids. There are also references to the fact that the stand was used for making square, and round cross-section braids, as well as being used for braiding with strips of fabric and metallic threads (Chabros & Batculuun 1993).

Examples of braid embroidery can be found in the countries bordering the west of China, but to date, there are no reports of the stand & bobbin braiding technique. Of the theme and variations found along the southern border, perhaps the best known is the braiding of the Lao Mien. Their work forms a subgroup of braiding that shares a common connection with the Chinese work; in particular to the metallic braids mentioned earlier (Fig. 8). The braids are applied onto their costume and accessories to form decorative borders to their designs. The stand & bobbin equipment consists of a large purpose-made basket, which is usually covered with fabric. There is no roller system. Instead the threads, and growing braid, are attached onto a small stick that is wedged into the top of the basket. The bobbins are similar to the Chinese ones. They are hook-ended

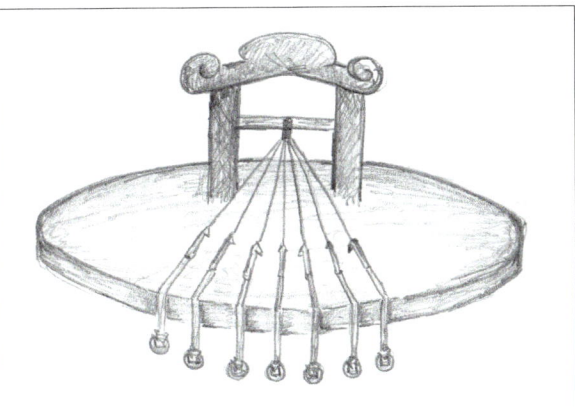

Fig. 25.
The Mongolian braiding stand and bobbins are very similar to the Dong equipment seen in Fig. 54. This drawing is based on research by Chabros and Batculuum (1993).

and weighted with coins, or other heavy objects such as nuts or washers.

Their work also illustrates that the exchange of ideas, and the spread of braiding, is still active today. Refugee Mien from Laos, now living in Thailand, have adapted their designs to incorporate traditional Thai motifs, whilst the local Thai people have adopted the traditional Lao Mien braiding technique and the design style (see Fig. 24).

By comparing the Chinese braid embroidery with textiles and techniques from different cultures, it can be seen that similarities exist. The exchange, and amalgamation, of foreign ideas could explain the connections. But without further evidence it would be difficult to clarify who was influencing whom.

Fig. 24.
Cushion covers from Thailand, decorated with braid around the edge of the motifs. The cover on the left, with a traditional Thai motif of an elephant, was made by refugee Lao Mien. The one on the right was inspired by traditional Lao Mien textiles, but was designed and made by indigenous Thai people.

Evolution & Change

Fig. 26.
Li Jinying comes from the Miao village of Wengxiang, near Kaili, Guizhou. She is demonstrating braidmaking using traditional stand and bobbin equipment. She uses the finished braids to decorate her costume, like the outfit she is wearing.

Evolution & Change

The Miao.

Today, braid embroidery is usually associated with the Miao minority,[21] one of the many ethnic groups that constitute the Chinese people. It has been suggested that the technique is unique to this ethnic group. However, many minority groups still use braids applied to decorate their costume, though not with the same abundance. The Miao costume varies dramatically from area to area, with different techniques and designs being attributed to different subgroups. Not all of the groups use braid embroidery, though Miao living in the Leishan, Kaili and Taijiang counties of East Guizhou are renowned for this work. Here, the appliqué is used to create particularly impressive decorative textiles.

The Miao appear to have retained many ancient skills, but it is hard to say how their production, and use, of braid has changed over the centuries. The earliest datable example of Miao costume[22] is of a type that does not incorporate braid, so a direct comparison cannot be made. Early photographic material is another source for consideration. By comparing the

Fig. 27.
There is a wide range of Miao textiles, though similarities can be seen within the various subgroups. The detail below is from a festival jacket from the Taijiang region, an area renowned for braid embroidery.

Evolution & Change

pictures with today's clothing, it appears that traditional costume has retained many of the patterns and designs found in earlier examples. Unfortunately, photographic evidence is not clear enough to distinguish technical details. It is possible that although the designs have remained the same, the techniques used to create them have changed. Indeed this seems likely as various comments suggest. For example, Smith (2005:18) says "An old lady told me that aprons in Shidong Township used to be woven before the Cultural Revolution. Nowadays, they are embroidered as the young lack the weaving skills and embroidery is considered easier." In fact, this process of simplifying the technique, whilst retaining the design style, is still continuing, as can be seen in the textiles shown on pages 32 and 33.

It is uncertain quite why the braid embroidery work is so intricate and prevalent in the Leishan, Kaili and Taijiang regions. The Miao in this area are relatively affluent compared to their more rural kinsfolk. In the past, they appear to have had more access to external trade, and exposure from outside influences. This is reflected in their textiles, which generally show more variety in technique and material than other Miao groups (Smith 2005:8).

One reason why braid embroidery has persisted longer with the Miao than with other groups could be due to the fact that costume plays an important part in Miao culture. Traditionally, their costume is their main form of decorative display, and its significance is many fold. For example, in the absence of a Miao written language,[23] their textiles are said to illustrate stories of their past, with each part of the design having meaning.[24] The costume also acts as a signifier, identifying the wearer as belonging, not just to the Miao minority, but to a particular group within the Miao. In addition, it visually defines the wearer's wealth and status. The quality of the textile, as well as the time and resources invested in a costume, are recognised and valued in Miao culture. This has a direct relationship to the appreciation of the skill of the Miao women who make the textiles. Indeed Corrigan (2001:11) writes "It is said that unmarried Miao girls are judged by their future husbands on their ability to spin, weave, embroider and make an elaborate costume, the beauty and workmanship of which indicates their tenacity and industriousness." These skills have been passed down, verbally and visually, through generations of female family members, forming the basis of a girl's education. Typically, the whole process of textile production, from raw material to finished garment, is learnt by each Miao woman. The self-sufficient nature of this process means that all the materials are manufactured and used within the home environment, without the need for commercial exchange. Customarily, the finished garments are also outside of market forces, having been made for the maker's own use, or for her family. However, this picture of Miao textiles is no longer prevalent.

Fig. 28 (opposite page).
Four Miao braidmakers from Guizhou (clockwise from top left). Li Zheng from Xijiang, Leishan County. Lisheng Ying from Mali, Taijiang County. 13-year old Pan Sheng Feng from Jidae, Leishan County. Xiong Guiyang from Langde, Leishan County.

Evolution & Change

Evolution & Change

Today & Tomorrow.

There seems to be an overwhelming agreement that life in China has undergone a radical transformation since the 1980's. There are many reasons for this, including political movement, economic reform, changes in education, tourist activity, and access to global influences. The repercussions of these changes filter down to affect even the technique of braid embroidery. Laumann (1993:23) sums up the widely held view of how these changes are effecting the Miao textiles, "Handicrafts are gradually being replaced by machines, homemade fabrics by factory-made textiles, natural dyes by chemical dyes, and the ways of making clothes are being replaced by coarse workmanship. The Miao's sense of values is also changing: young people are beginning to doubt their own culture and traditional beliefs. They are not willing to spend a great deal of time on weaving, dyeing and embroidery; their rich culture is becoming engulfed by modern economical concerns, and the pictorial symbols are disappearing." It could be argued that these changes are not a new phenomenon, but part of an on going process. This comment, from the 1920's, quoted by Rossi (1987:30) makes an interesting comparison. "The Ch'uan Miao men no longer wear embroidered garments and the women are imitating, to save time, the styles of the Chinese embroideries... The change is taking place so fast that the difference between the clothing worn now and even two years ago is quite noticeable... Within 20 years there will probably be no such embroideries among the

Fig. 29 (above).
The Miao still continue their traditional agricultural work, farming the upper regions of Guizhou.

Fig. 30 (left)
Washing in the river, surrounded by electricity lines and satellite dishes, in Xijiang, Leishan County, Guizhou.

Evolution & Change

Ch'uan Miao."

This sense of a transformation is not restricted to just China. Similar incidents can be seen in other cultures, and across the spectrum of time. Although the 'new' can be assimilated, it is often associated with the loss of the 'old'. Attitudes and fashions are constantly adapting and absorbing new ideas. New techniques and materials are accepted and adjusted. Even the 'old' is periodically revived.

Today, the situation continues, with certain aspects moving faster than others. Braid making is such a time-consuming activity, and the results so minute, that it is not surprising to find that it is no longer a widespread craft. Even within the realms of the Miao, it is becoming increasingly scarce. Interviews, conducted in 2005, revealed a common theme. Most of the women braidmakers were over the age of 50 years. Whilst they continued to make and use braids, their daughters did not, in spite of the fact that they knew how to. Meanwhile, the granddaughters were not even learning how to braid, as the emphasis is now on a more formal education. Several of the older women commented that their mothers had known more braid patterns than they did. Of course there are exceptions, but the trend seems to be towards the gradual loss of textile skill in favour of other, more academic, abilities.

The demand for braids has decreased in two aspects. Firstly, the more ornate, braid-consuming styles of couching down are appearing less frequently. Traditional Miao costume is no longer viewed as the main expression of a woman's status and ability. So, if the effort involved in producing an exquisite piece of work is not fully appreciated, then there is little incentive to invest the time in its fabrication. Faster solutions for interpreting the designs, such as flat, rather than 3-dimensional, appliqué, seem to be accepted. In more and more cases, the braid embroidery is being imitated with alternative techniques and materials; a trend that is even more apparent in the textiles produced by other minority groups. Examples show that the handmade braid has been replaced with machine-made braids and cords, and the effect of braid embroidery has been mimicked with hand stitching, and even machine embroidery. This reduction in the use of braid appliqué on traditional costume is compounded by the general decline in the making, and wearing, of handmade textiles. Western fashions are becoming more popular, and machine-made garments are becoming the norm.

However, a new market for the Miao textiles has developed. The increase in tourism has opened up the possibility of textile items being sold as souvenirs. The Miao are renowned for their costume, so this is one of the attributes that is highlighted as an attraction. Many tourists from China, as well as from abroad, come to Guizhou to visit the Miao villages. Here they expect to see Miao 'tradition', in the form of a staged display of music and dance by participants wearing typical Miao costume. So increasingly, the display of costume is for a wider audience, with the emphasis on an overall visual effect. As the significance of the costume changes, so does the relevance of the finer detail. The value and appreciation of the time-consuming textile skills is no longer the focus of attention, so quicker alternatives are readily accepted. Yet the skills still retain some merit. Demonstrations of textile techniques are also offered as a tourist attraction, so they continue to have some worth. Small items, such as purses and bags, are also produced especially for the tourist market. And so, the tradition of Chinese braid embroidery continues to evolve, adapting to suit the demands of today's society.

Evolution & Change

Fig. 31 (top left).
Old Laohan shoes from Tianlong village, Pingba county, Guizhou.

Fig. 32 (top right).
Detail showing the handmade braid, which is typical of the Laohan work.

Fig. 33 (left).
Detail of a new pair of shoes from the same village. This modern interpretation of the braid is made from strands of machine-made tubular knitting.

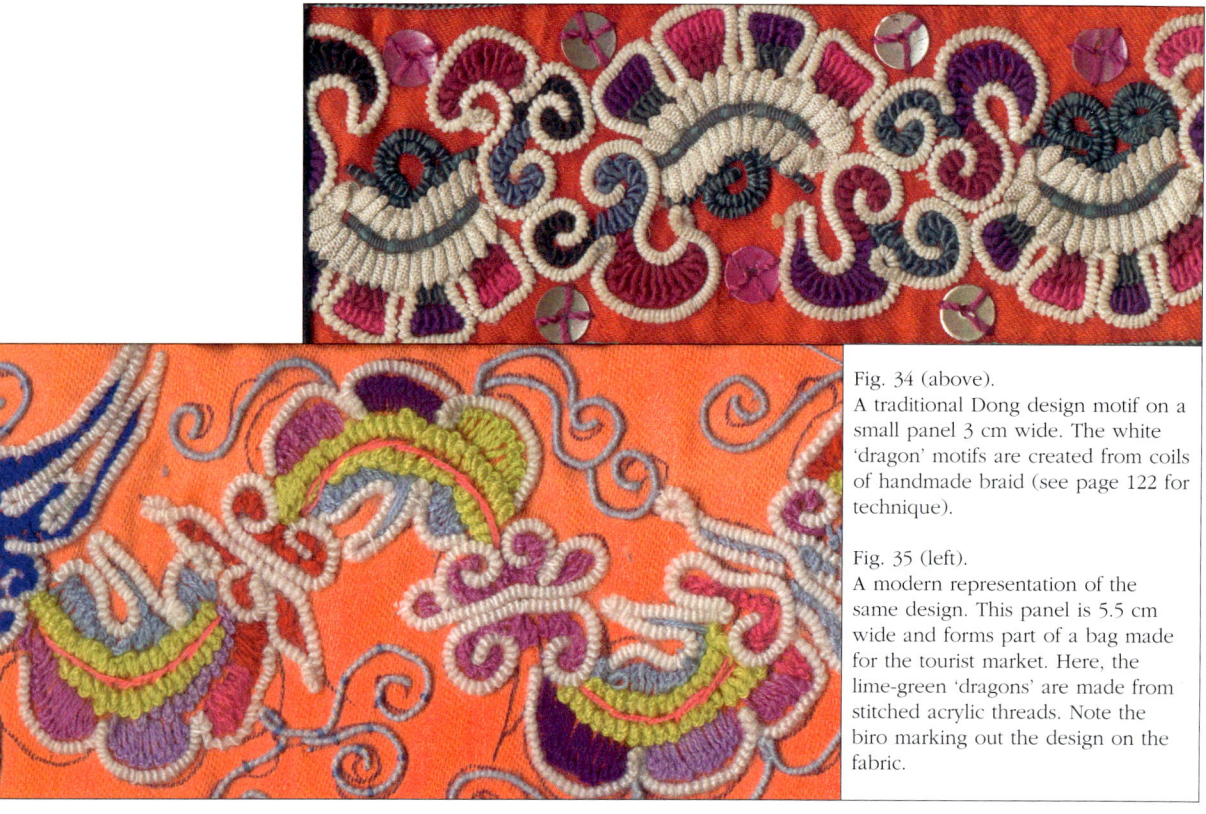

Fig. 34 (above).
A traditional Dong design motif on a small panel 3 cm wide. The white 'dragon' motifs are created from coils of handmade braid (see page 122 for technique).

Fig. 35 (left).
A modern representation of the same design. This panel is 5.5 cm wide and forms part of a bag made for the tourist market. Here, the lime-green 'dragons' are made from stitched acrylic threads. Note the biro marking out the design on the fabric.

Evolution & Change

Fig. 36.
This modern panel was purchased at Kaili market. It is a typical Miao design, and it is intended for use as a decorative sleeve panel on a festival jacket. However, its method of production is not traditional. Whereas old versions were handmade, using braid embroidery, this example is all machine stitched.
Courtesy of Ruth Smith.

Materials & Equipment

Braiding Threads.

A common theme running through textile production in southwest China is the self-sufficient nature of the work, with all the materials and equipment being produced within the near vicinity of the villages. But photographic evidence and oral history suggests that this has altered dramatically in the past few decades. Silk is still the main material used for braid embroidery, but local sericulture has declined. Instead, threads are purchased from market stall vendors. They supply a huge range of pre-dyed 2-ply silk, which is sold by weight. The silk is sold in tiny skeins, each weighing around half a gramme and providing roughly ten metres of silk. These small skeins, of a single

Fig. 38 (above).
The Miao often use old paperback books for storage. This image shows a spread of items found in one book and includes shoe templates, silk threads, finished braids and personal photographs.

Fig. 37 (below).
A market stall in Kaili City, Guizhou. Tiny skeins of silk are knotted together into large bundles, and laid out for display.

Materials & Equipment

Fig. 39 (above).
A Dong 'pocket' book, made from fabric and handmade paper that has been painted and varnished. The origami-style folded paper can be opened to reveal hidden compartments. It is used for storing skeins of silk, braid and other sundry items.

colour, are knotted together to make large bundles for display. Although 2-ply silk still remains the thread of choice, examples using a fine 3-ply, and chunkier synthetic fibres have also been found (for example see Fig. 105) Purchases are normally made in small quantities, as and when required. This explains the occasional mismatch of colour when threads run out. The Miao usually store these small skeins, and other sundry items, between the pages of an old book, whilst the Dong[23] use purpose-made containers created from intricately folded paper pockets.

Fig. 40 (below).
Customers help the vendor untangle a single skein from a large bundle of silk. Kaili City, Guizhou.

Materials & Equipment

Materials & Equipment

Braiding Stands.

There is a huge variety of braiding stands being used today. Made-for-purpose stands range from the ornately decorated, to the more rustic and robust. Other domestic items, such as baskets and buckets, are also commandeered to act as braiding stands. The purpose-made ones vary in style, though similarities can be seen in stands from particular areas. Generally, the Miao equipment is more makeshift, having been made from local materials, usually by male family members. The older stands that have survived are of the more ornate type, no doubt due to the fact that the plainer ones are less likely to be looked after. For example, Li Jinying said that the stand she learnt on was made for her grandmother, by her grandfather, but when it become old it was burnt. Old stands are scarce in Western collections, though examples have been found that originated from Anhui and Shanxi Provinces. Ornate stands are appearing in antique shops in places like Beijing and Shanghai, and they have even been found for sale on e-bay. These stands are marketed as 'footbinding' stools. The most decorative ones are beautifully carved and finished with red lacquer and gilded ornament.

In spite of the variations in style, there are basic features that unite all the stands. There are three main sections: the base, the working surface, and the roller system.

The base is used to raise the working surface to a comfortable height. Most of the braiding stands in use today have a base of around 50 to 60 cm in height. They are designed so that they are a comfortable height for the braidmaker, who works whilst seated on a small stool, which is approximately 15 to 20 cm in height (see Fig. 44). However, amongst the older, more ornate stands, it is not uncommon to find lower, table top versions.

The simplest stands have a base comprising three legs, made from wood that has

Fig. 41 (opposite page).
A Miao stand from Kaili City, Guizhou. The 3-legged base is a little higher than average, lifting the circular working surface 64 cm above the floor. The working surface varies between 31 and 32 cm in diameter, and has been varnished like the rest of the stand. The roller system, which is 23.5 cm high, sits slightly towards the rear of the circle and leans backwards. It consists of two carved uprights, a carved horizontal support and a cylindrical roller bar. The top of the roller bar sits 15 cm above the working surface and 24 cm from the front circumference. It is jammed with a small bamboo stick that is inserted through both the roller and the top support bar. The finished braid is attached to the roller bar with the working threads wound onto eight bamboo bobbins that pivot on the circumference of the working surface. They are weighted with marbles wrapped in pieces of silk felt.
Courtesy of Deanie Neuhofer.

Fig. 42.
Miao stands are usually made by a male family member, using local resources. Here, Mr. Li, from Wengxiang, demonstrates how he used a saw to cut the circular working surface, having marked an edge with a pencil attached to a piece of string and a nail.

Materials & Equipment

Fig. 43.
Fabric has been wrapped around this Miao roller bar to prevent the rough wood from snagging the silk threads.

been whittled by hand. The three-legged stands are usually supported with a horizontal T-bar, though there seems to be no preference as to whether the T faces away from or towards the worker. It is not uncommon to find a strip of fabric, or a cord, attached to the legs. This is used to hang the stand up out of the way whilst it is in storage. The more elaborate stands often have four legs. They usually display better carpentry skills, sometimes with decorative fretwork or reliefwork. Many of these stands have drawers, or cupboards, incorporated into the base, thus providing the perfect storage space for bobbins and other sundry items.

The working surface is attached to the top of the base. The flat surface is usually circular, although there are examples that are D-shaped, with a straight edge at the back and a semicircular edge at the front (see Fig. 44). Most surfaces measure between 30-40 cm in diameter. Only the edge of the flat surface is used,[25] so the horizontal area within the circumference is sometimes covered in decorative carvings. The working surface functions by providing an edge on which the braiding bobbins can rest. Ideally, the outer edge should be smooth, to minimise the possibility of snagging the silk threads. However, the makeshift nature of some of the stands does mean that this is not always the case. Some stools have been found with indentations on the front circumference (see Fig. 49). These have been deliberately carved into the edge and carefully smoothed down. They can be used to locate the bobbins around the working surface, although to date, stools of this type have not been seen in action.

The roller system sits vertically upwards from the back half of the working surface. Quite a few are angled so that they tilt slightly backwards. Some are detachable, making them easier to store when not in use. At minimum, the roller system consists of two upright bars, strengthened with a horizontal bar that connects them together. Also sitting between the two uprights is the roller bar, consisting of a cylindrical rod that can turn. The roller can sit above, or below the support bar, or even between the supports if there are two horizontal bars. Once again, the superior versions are beautifully finished, and can be shaped and carved. The most intricate have carved panels, or fretwork, instead of support bars. They can even have additional decorative features, such as the carved creatures seen in Fig. 53.

Fig. 44 (opposite page).
A Miao stand from Wengxiang, near Kaili, Guizhou. The braider sits on the small wooden stool whilst working at this 3-legged stand. The robust roller system tilts away from the front of the D-shaped working surface.

Materials & Equipment

Materials & Equipment

The height of the roller bar, and its distance from the front edge of the working surface, affects the tensioning of the braid. However, there seems to be little conformity in these measurements. An average height of the roller bar is between 10 - 20 cm from the working surface. The function of the roller bar is to allow the braiding to be a continuous process. A short length of spare thread is tied onto the centre of the bar. This is used to attach the silk threads onto the roller bar. As the silk threads are worked together, the braid gradually grows away from the bar. The end of the braid, where the threads are actually interlacing together, is known as the 'point of braiding'. This must remain away from the circumference of the working surface, in order for the braiding to progress. By gradually winding the braid onto the roller bar, the point of braiding can be kept at the correct height, away from the edge of the working surface. As the roller bar is also used to store the finished braid, it needs to be smooth to prevent the threads from snagging. Sometimes strips of fabric, or paper, are wrapped around the rougher equipment, to protect the finished braid (see Fig. 43 for an example.

On the more sophisticated systems, there is a small handle that projects out beyond one of the uprights. This is used to rotate the roller when the braid is being wound on. On the other stools, the roller bar is simply wound directly. Some form of jamming device is needed to stop the roller bar from unwinding. This is done in several ways, all of which require holes pierced into the roller bar. The number of holes and the diameter of the bar all affect the tensioning of the braid, with better results obtained from holes that sit closer together around the circumference of the roller. A wooden, or metal, stick is placed into one of these holes and allowed to rest against the horizontal support bar, thus preventing the roller bar from moving further. The stick will either rest against the back, or the front of the horizontal bar, depending on which way the braid has been wound onto the roller, and whether the roller is above or below the support. Although both instances have been observed, it is more common to see the braid coming up, over the top of the roller bar, and down towards the front of the stand.

Fig. 45 (above).
Ordinary household objects can be adapted into braiding equipment. Here, a bucket is utilised with Dong bobbins. Pingzai Village, Liping County, Guizhou.
Courtesy of Ien Rappoldt.

Fig. 46 (left).
Baskets are also used as improvised braiding stands.

Materials & Equipment

Some roller systems have an extra hole situated in the horizontal support, directly above the holes in the roller. The stick can then be passed through the horizontal bar and down into the roller bar (see Fig. 41 for an example). Fig. 47 shows a novel approach for jamming the roller. Here, the stick is held by a piece of string. This is attached to the top of the roller system and is pulled taut, jamming the stick in place, away from the wooden framework. A couple of old stands did not need the jamming sticks as the roller bar was stiff enough to stay in place. However, it is thought that the stiffness was due to lack of use, rather than by design, as the roller bars still had holes in them ready to accommodate a stick.

So far, the equipment described has been especially made for the purpose. However, household items are adapted to serve as substitutes. The wooden bucket, shown in Fig. 45. has had a roller bar added and a jamming stick has been inserted through a hole drilled into the bucket's handle. More often it is a basket that is improvised into a braiding stand. The wide rim of the basket provides the working edge on which the bobbins rest. The handle acts as a support onto which a roller bar can be lashed into place. Sometimes the braid is attached directly to the handle.

Fig. 48 (above).
A typical example of a jamming stick inserted through the roller bar. It rests against the support bar, preventing the roller bar from moving.

Fig. 47 (right).
A Miao braiding stand from Taijiang County, Guizhou. A jamming stick prevents the roller bar from moving. This unusual example is pulled taut, away from the top support bar, by a piece of string.

Materials & Equipment

Materials & Equipment

Fig. 49 (opposite page).
An ornate stand, with a drawer incorporated into the base. It is embellished with gilded and red lacquered decorative features. The working surface is approximately 35 cm in diameter and has 18 indents around the front circumference. The central roller sits about 18 cm above the surface and has a small handle extending beyond the upright supports. Although there is no jamming device, there are small holes in the roller where one would normally sit. This particular stand was bought as a 'footbinding' stool, although there appears to be no evidence that they were used for this purpose.
From the collection of Beverley Jackson. Photography by Larry Kunkel.

Fig. 50 (above).
A Dong braiding stand incorporating a shelf in the base. The diameter of the working surface is approximately 38 cm, and supports an ornate roller system. Decorative fretwork and carved panels surround the central roller, which sits about 15 cm above the working surface. The roller has a handle which extends out beyond the upright supports. The ten bone bobbins are weighted with fabric sacks containing small stones.

Materials & Equipment

Fig. 51 (above).
An unusual Miao stand found in Taijiang city. The working surface has been covered with fabric. A screw driver, inserted through holes in the top support bar, makes an inventive solution to jamming the roller bar in place. The slit-top bamboo bobbins are weighted with metal nuts.

Fig. 52 (left).
This Miao stand, from Taijiang County, has an unusual pedestal base. The roller has a simple wire handle extending beyond the uprights, which are supported by two horizontal bars. The bamboo bobbins are weighted with metal washers and a few old coins.

Materials & Equipment

Fig. 53 (above).
A detached roller system from a Dong stand. The uprights, which slot into holes on the working surface, are joined with carved decorations and topped with dragons. Threads wound onto bobbins are still attached to the roller bar.

Fig. 54 (right).
Another beautifully carved Dong stand, with a drawer incorporated into the base. This one has a smaller working surface, with a diameter of approximately 25 cm. The working surface is also carved with floral designs and supports typical Dong bobbins.

Materials & Equipment

Braiding Bobbins.

The threads, attached to the roller bar, are wound onto bobbins that rest around the circumference of the working surface. The bobbins serve many purposes. Firstly, they act as a storage system, allowing long lengths of thread to be worked with ease. As the bobbins are weighted, they also provide a tension on the thread. This helps to maintain a smooth and even pull on the threads as they interlace together, thus resulting in a neater braid. The bobbins protect the threads as well. By manipulating the bobbins, rather than the threads, the handling of the fibres is reduced. The wear and tear is further diminished because it is the bobbins, not the threads, which rub against the working surface. In addition, the bobbins help with the actual braiding procedure, by keeping the threads in position and in the correct order.

There are many different types of bobbins, though similarities can be found in bobbins that originate from the same area. The most common kind of Miao bobbin in use today, is made from a thin stick of bamboo. This plant grows readily around the Miao villages, so the materials are freely available. The average bobbin is about 0.5 cm in diameter, and 15 to 20 cm in length. Most bobbins have a hook feature at the top. This is used to stop the thread from unravelling off the bobbin. The hook is made from a small branch of bamboo that is left protruding from a node at the base of the main stalk. When the bamboo is used upside-down, the branch points downwards forming a natural hook (see Fig. 55). Some Miao bobbins utilise a slit in the main bamboo stalk. This style of securing is very firm. Although the slits can be a little rough, the bobbins are less likely to tangle with each other, as they do not have protruding hooks. Larger stems of bamboo are also used to make bobbins. Here, only part of the outer circumference is used. It can be shaped to form flatter bobbins, such as the Bouyei[26] ones seen in Fig. 59.

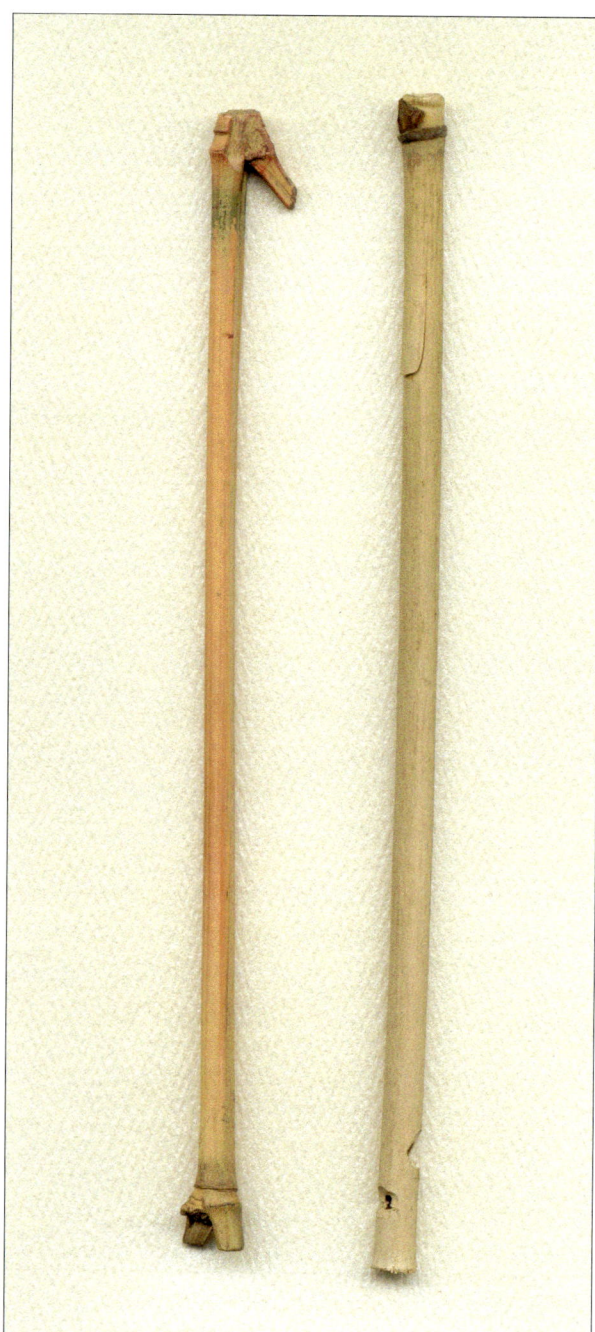

Fig. 55.
Miao bobbins are usually made from bamboo. These bobbins are approximately 18 cm in length. Typically, a single branch is left protruding from a node on the main stalk, so that it forms the hook for securing the thread (seen on the left). In some cases the bobbins are made from just a straight stalk of bamboo. A small cut is sliced into the stalk near the top of the bobbin. This provides a slit that can be used to stop the thread unravelling. The holes at the base of the bobbins are for attaching the weight (seen on the right).

Materials & Equipment

Fig. 56.
These slit-topped bobbins are approximately 16 cm long, and are wound ready for action. A notch cut into the base of the bobbin allows a tie to be threaded through the hollow bamboo. This is used to attach the washers, that act as weights. Taijiang County, Guizhou.

Materials & Equipment

Weights are added onto the bottom of the bobbins. They are attached with a piece of thick thread, or even a short length of the silk braid, which is knotted either directly onto the shank of the bobbin, or through a small hole near its base. Today, the weights are often made from ceramic shapes. They are usually roughly fashioned, although some are beautifully glazed. All sorts of other items have also been found loading the bobbins, including coins, metal nuts and washers, medicine phials, and even children's toys. A set of bobbins is normally weighted with the same type of object, so that they provide a similar tension on each thread. However, because the type of object varies considerably from set to set, the average weight of a bobbin ranges between 15 to 30 grammes.

Bone bobbins are normally associated with the Dong minority, although the Miao from Taijiang use distinctive bone bobbins (see Fig. 58). The Dong bobbins (see Fig. 61) are made from flat sections of ox bone that have been shaped into hooks with a hole pierced through the lower end. They are around 5

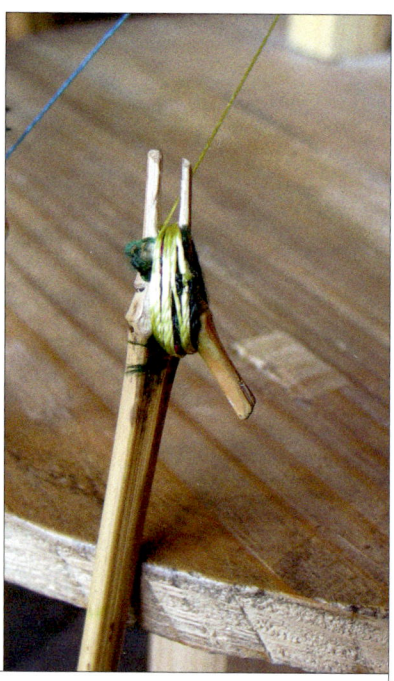

Fig. 57 (above).
Detail of a bamboo bobbin from Xijiang, Leishan County, Guizhou. The bobbin has an additional prong shape carved into the main stalk. This enables the silk to be wrapped around the bobbin in a different way, imitating the bone bobbins seen below.

Fig. 58 (below).
Miao bobbins made from buffalo bone, from the Taijiang area. The bobbins are about 14 cm long with oval cross-sections approximately 6 by 4 mm diameter. The unusual shaped heads are about 3 cm by 1.5 cm. Fabric sacks, full of rice, have been stitched onto the ends of the bobbins. Each bobbin weighs approximately 30 gm.

Materials & Equipment

to 6 cm in length and 1 cm in width, narrowing towards the neck of the hook. A weight is made from a quantity of stones, or rice, contained inside a square fabric package, approximately 4 to 5 cm in width. Typically the weight is around 25 to 30 grammes. The fabric packages are often made from indigo-dyed, plain-weave cotton and feature a small loop of fabric at the top of the square. The loop provides a means of attaching a tie that is then connected to the hole in the bone bobbin. The ties are relatively long, making the weight hang between 10 and 15 cm away from the base of the bobbin. The ties are made from twisted cords or strips of fabric and can easily be replaced if they start to wear. The reason they might wear is because it is the tie, rather than the bone bobbin, which rests on the edge of the working surface. The movement of this style of bobbin is quite different from the longer bamboo ones (see page 59).

Fig. 59 (left).
This Bouyei bobbin is beautifully carved from the outer surface of a large bamboo stalk. It is almost flat, and measures approximately 20 cm long and 1 cm wide. A ceramic shape weights the bobbin to about 40 grams.

Fig. 60 (below).
The hook-ended Bouyei bobbins in action, in Huishi County, Guizhou.
Courtesy of Gina Corrigan.

Materials & Equipment

Fig. 61 (above).
A selection of Dong ox-bone bobbins ranging between 4.5 cm and 6.5 cm in length. This style of bobbin is flat with a carved hook end. The hole pierced into the base is for attaching the weight bag tie.

Fig. 62 (left).
An old Dong stand, originally from Liping County. Fabric sacks are filled with small stones to provide the weight, and are joined onto the bobbins by a fabric strip. The detail (below) shows the strip of fabric stitched into the bobbin's hole.

Materials & Equipment

Fig. 63 (above).
Typical Miao bobbins made from bamboo stalks with hooks formed from small branches. They are weighted with unglazed ceramic shapes, tied onto the bamboo with lengths of silk braid. These bobbins are approximately 15 cm long and weigh around 30 gm each. Wengxiang, near Kaili, Guizhou.

Fig. 64 (left).
A glazed ceramic weight tied onto a Miao bobbin, from Langde, Leishan County. It weighs about 17 gm.

Materials & Equipment

Fig. 65 (left).
All sorts of objects are used to weight the bobbins, such as these medicinal phials found in use in Leishan County.

Fig. 66 (below).
A novel use for ceramic toy whistles, that take the shape of zodiac animals. The average weight of the bobbins is around 21 gm.

Fig. 67 (far left).
Detail of a bobbin from Fig. 41. A single marble is wrapped in silk felt (this is made by silk worms extruding their silk over a flat surface, rather than into a cocoon). The bobbins weigh just 8 gm each. Kaili City, Guizhou.

Fig. 68 (left).
Here, two marbles have been wrapped in fabric and attached onto the shank of the bobbin. The bobbin's total weight is just 12 grammes.

Materials & Equipment

Fig. 69.
Old Chinese coins are ideally suited for bobbin weights. People often associate them with the braiding bobbins, but they are not particularly common. This could be due to the fact that they have a higher commercial value than the washers and ceramic weights that are normally used today. Modern reproduction coins, such as these found on Miao bobbins, are available from the market.
Courtesy of Ien Rappoldt.

Materials & Equipment

Fig. 70.
A lady selling paper templates on the street corner on market day. Taijiang City.

Materials & Equipment

Paper Templates.

Braid embroidery can be as simple as a straight edge, bordering other decorative stitching and textile work. The more intricate braid embroidery is worked into symbolic motifs. Paper templates provide a guide to these designs. They are made in a batch by cutting through a pile of paper sheets that are held together with small plugs of paper. The sheets are then separated and sold to individuals who interpreted the pattern using their own choice of colours, materials and techniques. Because the same paper motifs are repeated many times, there is still a continuity and cohesive style to costume from certain areas. The paper templates are glued directly onto the surface of the panels. The braid is then couched down over the top of the paper, and

Fig. 71.
The reverse of a template intended for a baby carrier. It shows that this one has been made from recycled note paper. It is about 14 cm by 15 cm square.

the template will remain in place when the work has been completed. Examples have been found where the expense of using a paper template has been avoided and the design has been drawn directly onto the fabric with a biro pen (see Fig. 35).

Fig. 72.
Two paper templates for large sleeve panels destined for festival jackets. The top one measures 19 cm x 33 cm and the other is 24 cm x 33 cm. These typical Miao designs will be secured onto the fabric to act as a guide for the braid embroidery. The patterns depict myths and symbolic motifs. Taijiang County, Guizhou.

Materials & Equipment

Fabric.

The braid embroidery is usually worked as a decorative feature on a small fabric panel. Some panels are less than 10 cm wide, and they are usually no larger than 20 to 30 cm square. When the decorative work is finished, the panels are then added onto larger items such as jackets and baby carriers. This method, of working small sections, makes the embroidery work more portable and easier to stitch. The panels are usually made from layers of fabric. Traditionally, the fabrics were handwoven locally. Although some home-production continues, machine-made fabrics are widely available at the markets and are more commonly used. Typically, the panels consist of a silk satin surface fabric, with a base of plain-weave, cotton or bast fibre stiffened with paper and paste. The layers are stitched together to form a firm base onto which the braids are applied. The small sections are usually firm enough to work in the hand, without a support or frame. Although sometimes bamboo splints are used to support the work.

Fig. 73.
Detail showing the layers of fabric on a panel.

Materials & Equipment

Needles & Thread.

The other main requirement for the appliqué work, apart for a ready supply of braids, is a needle and thread. Fine needles are used, in keeping with the delicate nature of the braids. They are sold at market in small, folded paper packs. The thread used for the stitching is usually the same type of silk used for the braiding, though it is not often the same shade. In fact, it is not uncommon to find that various colours have been used on one piece, suggesting that odds and ends have been used up for this purpose. The sewing threads can be conditioned with a bean paste. This strengthens the threads and makes them easier to work with. It can also be used for stiffening the fabric. The paste is made from the seeds of the locust bean tree. The dried beans are simmered in water until they form a jelly-like substance. This is then wrapped in a leaf, although today it is more likely to be contained in a small plastic bag. The threads are 'waxed' by piercing the threaded needle through the package so that the thread is drawn through the substance.

Fig. 74.
Sundry items belonging to Shidong Miao. The bundle of fine braid is rolled onto paper. It is less than 1 mm wide, and has approximately 14 stitches per cm. The pattern is the most common one found on Shidong items and will be stitched down as a straight border with the fine needle that can be seen inserted into the paper. The folded packets contain more needles that are just 1.5 cm long. The dried beans are from the locust bean tree. They are used to make a paste for conditioning the sewing threads.

Braiding

Introduction.

A supply of finished braids is needed before any appliqué work can commence. The embroiderer normally makes these for herself, although there appears to be a certain amount of flexibility with this. A braiding stool is often shared within a family group, and several members may contribute by making sections of one braid. This practice was observed, as well as mentioned in interviews, and it could explain the subtle changes in structure that can be found in some examples (see Fig. 75). Occasionally, braids are removed from old garments and reused on new items. However, old festival jackets, covered with silk braids, are usually overdyed in indigo in order to extend their useful life.

As the braiding actions are fairly large scale, they are not a strain on the eyesight. This means that braiding can continue into the

Fig. 76.
This bundle of braid has been made as one piece. At the start of the braid, all eight bobbins were loaded with pale blue silk. Gradually, as each thread came to an end it was replaced, with either red, green and turquoise silk.

Fig. 75.
This detail, from Fig. 103, shows a point at which there is a subtle change in the structure of the braid. The striped braid has a central line that switches from a right-over-left Z-join, to a left-over-right S-join (marked with the arrow). This could easily be caused when a different worker takes over the braidmaking.
Courtesy of Elizabeth Andrews.

Braiding

evening, when poor light would make stitching very difficult. The braids are made by moving the bobbins around the stool in set sequences. The order in which the bobbins travel under and over each other determines the final structure of the braid. Since it is the bobbins that are lifted, the equipment affects the feel of the process. The Miao bamboo bobbins pivot firmly on the working surface. This pivot action is transferred when the bobbins are lifted onto the fingers, giving a dynamic flow to movement of the bobbins. In comparison, the Dong bobbins feel floppy, but more stable, as they fall against the working surface. These differences will affect the way in which the bobbins are handled. Once the braiding method is mastered, a rhythmic action is achieved. Not only does this help to keep an even tension on the work, but it also speeds up the process.

The quality of the braid work varies considerably. Many of the braids found on old textiles are very fine, with an even tension. It is not uncommon to find braids less than 1 mm wide with between 25 and 30 stitches per cm along the edge. The better quality appliqué work tends to be made with firmly tensioned braids. Tight, uniform stitches are achieved by making smooth, even movements and by keeping the point of braiding at a steady position. This means that the braid needs to be frequently wound onto the roller bar, so that the place where the braid is actually formed stays at a similar distance from the bar. If the point of braiding is allowed to fluctuate from near the roller to close to the working surface, there will be a marked change in the tension when the braid is finally wound onto the roller (see Fig 77). The distance, and angle, between the roller bar and the working surface also affects the tension on the stitches. Today, the Miao seem untroubled with trying to achieve a uniform braid, and many of their braids have irregular tension. This rather carefree attitude to the braid's appearance can also be seen when the working threads are replaced. As the thread on a bobbin comes to an end, a new thread is knotted on and work continues. It is not uncommon to find that this new thread is of a completely different colour to the rest of the braid. This also demonstrates that there is little wastage of the precious silk (see Fig. 76).

Fig. 77.
Detail of a Miao panel. The green braid bordering the motif shows a marked change in tension from tight to loose stitches. This can be caused by sudden and infrequent winding of the braid onto the roller bar.
Courtesy of Gina Corrigan.

Braiding

Reading the Instructions.

There are many different braid structures used for Chinese braid embroidery. The following chapter details just a few braids. Each braid is explained with step-by-step instructions. These describe the moves that bobbins make during one sequence. The sequence must be repeated many times to create the braid. The bobbins are numbered at the start of the braiding row, to help identify each one. By the end of the row, the bobbins will be in different positions, so they will need mentally renumbering before using the text to work the next row. A summary of the sequence is also given. This should help provide a mental picture of the process, enabling the moves to be considered as a single continuous action. The first braid, JC1, is illustrated with detailed photographs to help establish the braiding method. The same process can then be applied to the subsequent braids. The action photographs are shown with a different coloured thread on each bobbin - this is simply to clarify the moves.

It should be noted that there are many ways of producing the same braid structure. The fact that different movements can sometimes result in the same structure can lay open the debate as to which is the 'correct' way. Observations in China have shown that different sequences are used to achieve the same structure, proving that there is more than one way being actively used today. Even when the same sequence is being worked, there are alternative ways of manipulating the bobbins (see Fig. 79). The instructions record just one method of working. However, they are open to interpretation if you wish to use another way. For example, some people find it easier to hold just one bobbin in each hand, rather than attempting to lift several (as shown in Fig. 85). As long as the bobbins follow the course shown in the summary, the actual way they achieve that path is adaptable. For example, if the summary of braid JC1 is followed, then bobbins 1 and 8 will be moved along the working surface, going towards the centre. They will work under and over the other bobbins before they cross over one another. These moves can be made by picking up just one bobbin at a time in each hand, whilst the others rest on the working surface. Ideally the actions should be as smooth as possible. The faster, more experienced, braidmakers work the whole sequence with their hands flowing as one continuous, fluid movement.

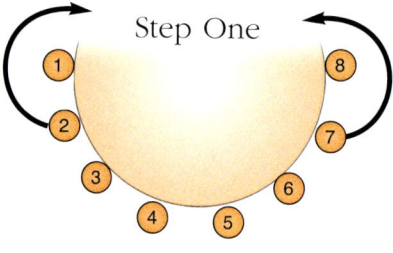

Fig. 78.
A diagrammatic view of the braiding process. The large partial circle represents the stand, with the smaller circles portraying the bobbins resting against its circumference. Each bobbin is numbered at the start of the sequence just to help clarify their route during the braiding moves. The arrows illustrate the path a bobbin must take to make a braiding move.

Adding More Thread.

If you wish to continue braiding and a thread is running out, you can add more. Simply unwind the old thread off the bobbin, and knot the end onto the start of a new one. Wind both threads back onto the bobbin and continue work. The knot is left in and gradually works its way into the braid.

Braiding

Getting Started.

Before braiding can commence, the stand needs to be prepared, and the bobbins wound with threads. The same method of preparation can be used, regardless of the type of equipment and the number of bobbins required. Usually, a single strand of silk thread is added onto each bobbin, but other alternatives can be tried.

1. Cut the required number of silk lengths, one for each bobbin. Knot the ends of these threads together with an overhand knot.

2. Tie the knot to the spare thread on the roller bar.

3. Check the jamming stick is in place before pulling out one strand of silk. Wind this thread onto the bobbin.

4. When the bobbin reaches the height of the working surface lay it down so that it rests against the edge. The hook at the top of the bobbin will prevent the silk from unravelling.

5. Repeat this process until each bobbin has been wound with silk. The equipment is now ready for braiding to commence.

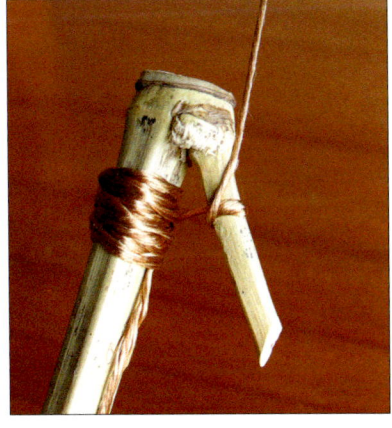

4a - some braiders added an extra turn around the hook for extra security.

4b - if you are using the notch style bobbins, the silk will need to be taken under the slit.

Braiding

Fig. 79.
There is no 'correct' way of manipulating the bobbins. This can be illustrated by the following photographs, which show several versions of the same move, all of which have been observed in China. This is the first move in most of the braiding sequences and shows bobbin 2 being lifted over bobbin 1.

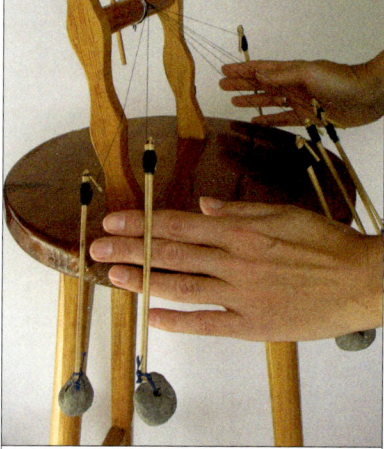

Fig. 79a.
The most common Miao version is to lift bobbin 2 on the back of all the fingers.

Fig. 79b.
An alternative is to lift the bobbin under the index finger and on the back of all others.

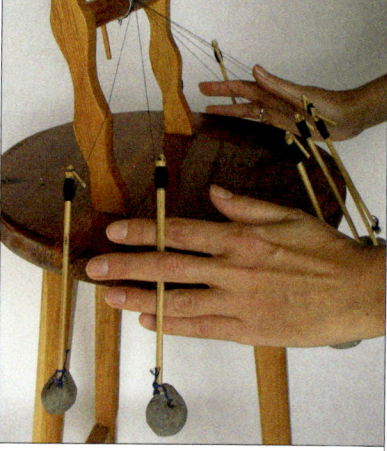

Fig. 79c.
Another similar action is to lift the bobbin under the middle finger and on the back of all others.

Fig. 79d.
This Dong version shows bobbin 2 flipped up with the thumb, whilst the fingers push bobbin 1 underneath it.

Fig. 79e.
Or, lift bobbin 2 with the thumb and index finger, whilst pushing bobbin 1 under it with the other three fingers.

Braid JC1

This is a 6-ridged, 8-bobbin flat braid. This single colour version is the most common braid used by the Miao today. It can be found stitched down in all forms of braid embroidery. This page shows the text and diagrams, whilst the step-by-step photographs can be found overleaf. The bobbins are identified by mentally numbering them 1 to 8, from left to right.

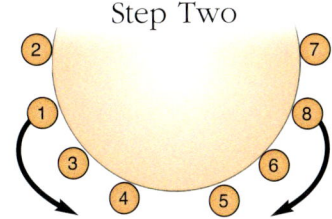

Step One.
Pick up bobbins 2 and 7 (on the backs of your fingers), and move them away from the centre, over bobbins 1 and 8. Drop bobbins 2 and 7 so that they are on the outside edges.

Step Two.
Lift bobbins 1 and 8 so that they are on the palm side of your fingers. Bring them towards the centre, over bobbins 3 and 6.

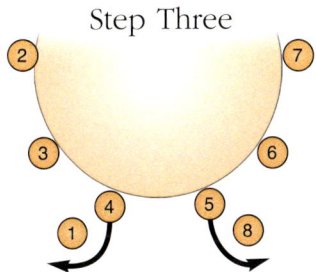

Step Three.
Continue lifting bobbins 1 and 8 on your fingers. Lift bobbins 4 and 5 onto the backs of your thumbs so that they sit above bobbins 1 and 8.

Step Four.
Continue lifting bobbins 4 and 5 on your thumbs and bring bobbin 1 and 8 towards the centre. Use your fingers to cross bobbin 8 over bobbin 1. Drop bobbins 8 and 1 so that they sit at the centre of the stand.

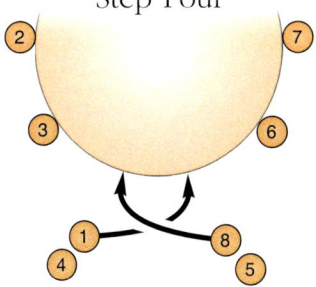

Step Five.
Drop bobbins 4 and 5 to the outside of bobbins 8 and 1.
You are now ready to start the sequence again.
The bobbins are all in different positions, so mentally renumber the bobbins 1 to 8 before using the written text.

Fig. 80.
Detail from a Miao panel with a 'looped' border made from Braid JC1.

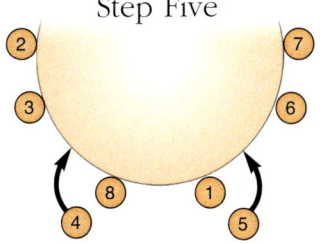

Braiding

Fig. 81.
Mentally number the bobbins 1 to 8. Here, they have been wound with different coloured threads to help identify each one.

Fig. 82.
Lift bobbins 2 and 7 on the backs of your hands and drop them over bobbins 1 and 8.

Fig. 83.
Pick up bobbins 1 and 8 between the thumb and fingers.

Fig. 84.
Bring bobbins 1 and 8 towards the centre, over bobbins 3 and 6.

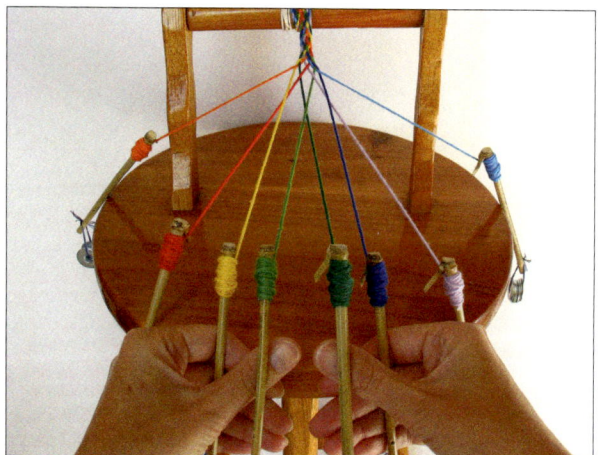

Fig. 85.
Continue lifting bobbins 1 and 8 on your fingers, and lift bobbins 4 and 5 onto the backs of your thumbs.

— 64 —

Braiding

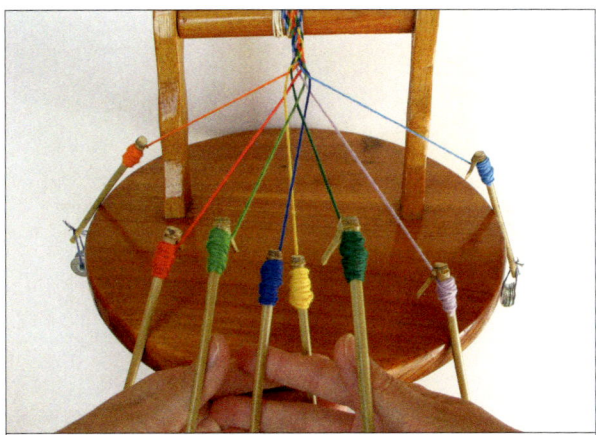

Fig. 86.
Continue lifting bobbins 4 and 5, so that they are above bobbins 1 and 8. Use your fingertips to take 8 over 1.

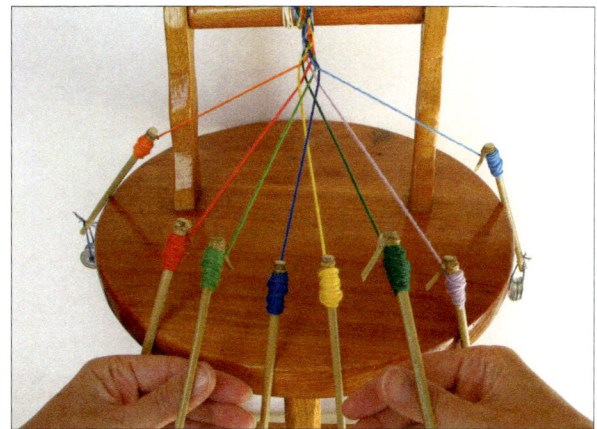

Fig. 87.
Drop bobbins 8 and 1 at the centre of the stand. Then drop bobbins 4 and 5 either side of them.

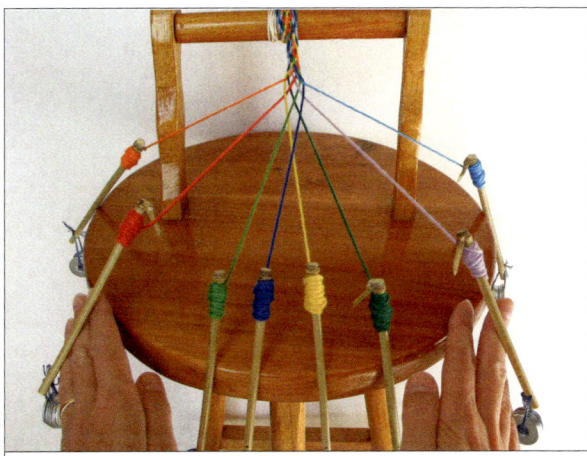

Fig. 88.
You are now ready to start the sequence again. The bobbins are all in different positions, so mentally renumber them before using the written text.

JC1 Summary.

The outermost bobbins go under one, over one, under one, then cross in the centre (right over left).

Tip - to improve the tension, keep the outside pair of bobbins spread well towards the back of the stand.

— 65 —

Braid JC2

This is the same structure as braid JC1, so the movements are identical. The chevron pattern is achieved by working with two colours of silk. Patterns are created on braid structures through the careful placement of colours at the start of the process. If the colours start in a different position, then a new pattern can be created. However, as the braiding sequence is worked, the colours will usually change position. Do not be concerned, as it is only the starting positions that are important. If an error is made in the sequence of moves, this can send the colours off in the wrong direction. You can either undo the mistake, or simply rearrange the colours back to their original positions, and start the braiding sequence again. There are many examples illustrating the latter of these options! To obtain the chevron pattern, the colours need to be arranged so that starting bobbins 1, 3, 6 and 8 are one colour, and bobbins 2, 4, 5 and 7 are another.

Fig. 89.
A Miao sleeve panel measuring 34 cm by 27 cm. The detail above shows an example of JC2. Cream and mauve silk threads have been braided together to create a chevron pattern. This example is just over 2 mm wide, and borders a motif filled with pleated braid.
Courtesy of Gina Corrigan.

Braid JC3

This is another version of braid JC1, so the movements are identical. Once again two colours of silk are used to obtain the pattern. However, the block pattern is achieved by having the colours start in different positions to that of JC2. Arrange the colours so that the starting bobbins 1, 2, 3 and 4 are one colour, and bobbins 5, 6, 7 and 8 are another colour.

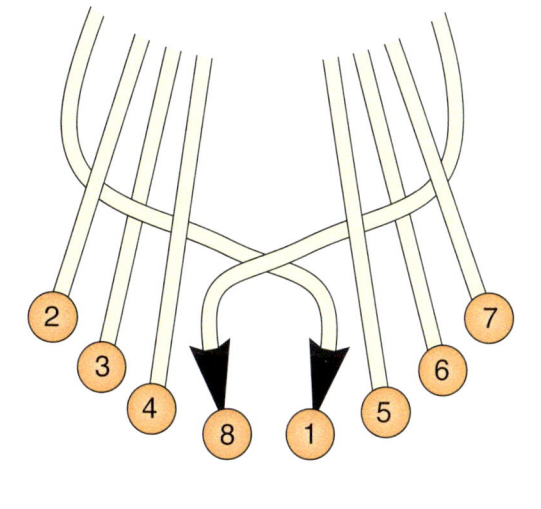

JC2 & JC3 Summary.

The outermost bobbins go under one, over one, under one, then cross in the centre (right over left).

Fig. 90.
This is a detail from the child's collar shown in Fig. 9. The pink and white block pattern is an example of JC3. It is created by placing the coloured threads in specific positions at the start of braiding.

Braid JC4

This 8-bobbin braid is made in the same manner as JC1, except an extra crossover is added at the centre. This twines the elements so that they head back to the edge of the braid from which they started. The resulting braid consists of two interlinked 4-bobbin braids. The two halves are usually worked in different colours creating a distinctive stripe pattern. This design is particularly effective for highlighting borders of a motif. It also gives an interesting result when used for 3-dimensional appliqué.

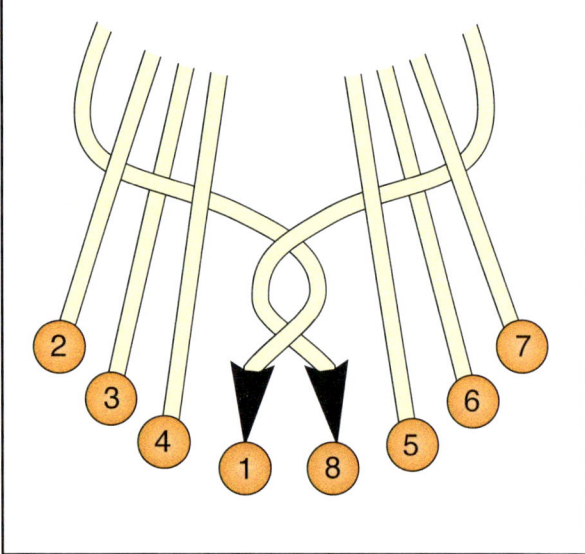

JC4 Summary.

The outermost bobbins go under one, over one, under one, then cross twice in the centre (right over left).

To make the stripe, start with bobbins 1, 2, 3 and 4 in one colour, and bobbins 5, 6, 7 and 8 in another.

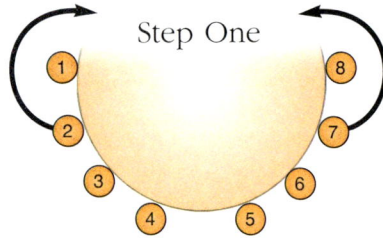
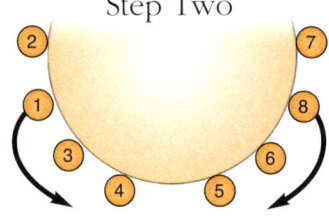
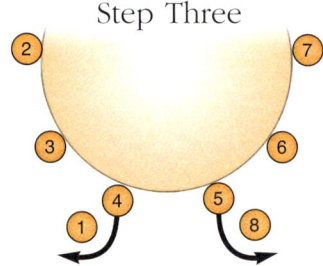

Step One.
Pick up bobbins 2 and 7 and move them away from the centre, over bobbins 1 and 8. Drop bobbins 2 and 7 so that they are on the outside edges.

Step Two.
Lift bobbins 1 and 8, and bring them towards the centre, over bobbins 3 and 6.

Step Three.
Continue lifting bobbins 1 and 8 on your fingers. Lift bobbins 4 and 5 onto the backs of your thumbs, so that they sit above bobbins 1 and 8.

Braiding

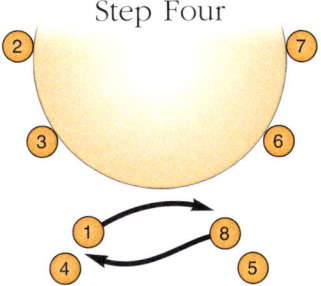 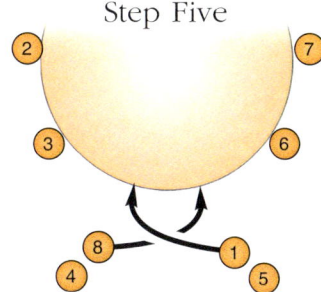 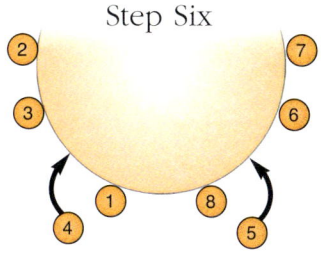

Step Four.
Continue lifting bobbins 4 and 5 on your thumbs and bring bobbin 1 and 8 towards the centre. Use your fingers to cross bobbin 8 over bobbin 1.

Step Five.
Continue lifting all four bobbins and cross bobbin 1 over 8. Then drop bobbins 1 and 8 so that they sit at the centre of the stand.

Step Six.
Drop bobbins 4 and 5 to the outside of bobbins 1 and 8.

Fig. 91.
A Miao festival jacket from Taijiang, Guizhou (pictured on the opposite page and detail above). Examples of braid JC4 are used to border some of the motifs.
Courtesy of Debbie James.

Braid JC5

This is an 8-bobbin braid, four of which interlace through the braid, parallel to the edges. The movements start like JC1, with the outer bobbins working towards the centre. However, at the centre the bobbins cross left over right, then work back out to the outer edge. This is one of the samples from the British Museum collection (see page 14). The design starts with bobbins 1, 3, 6 and 8 in white, and bobbins 2, 4, 5 and 7 in green.

JC5 Summary.

The outermost bobbins go under one, over one, under one, then cross in the centre (left over right). They then work towards the outer edge going over one and under one.

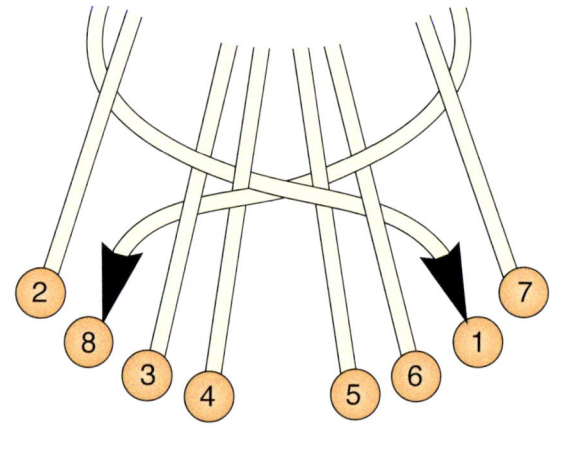

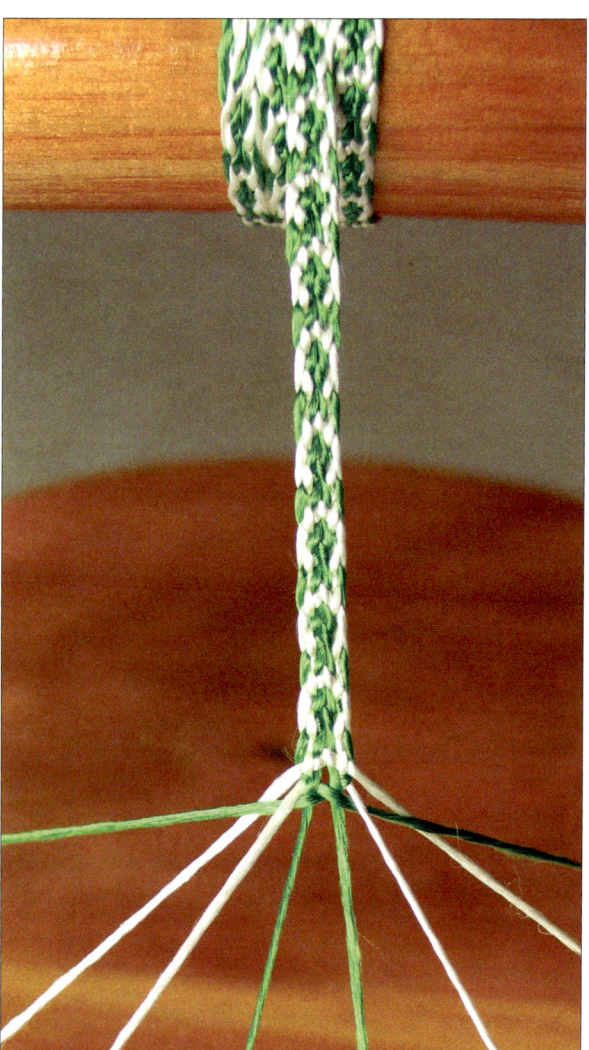

Fig. 92.
A reproduction of the braid sample found in the British Museum, and the braidmaking in progress (left).

Braiding

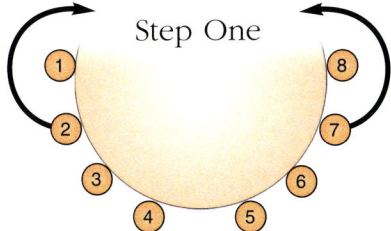
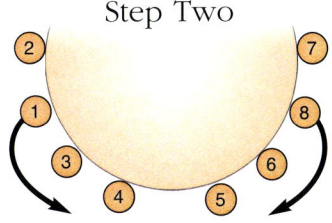
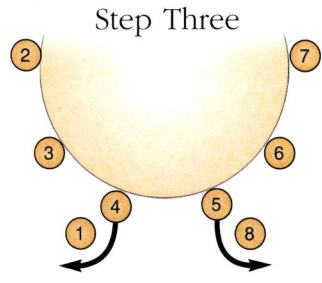

Step One.
Pick up bobbins 2 and 7 and move them away from the centre, over bobbins 1 and 8. Drop bobbins 2 and 7 so that they are on the outside edges.

Step Two.
Lift bobbins 1 and 8, and bring them towards the centre, over bobbins 3 and 6.

Step Three.
Continue lifting bobbins 1 and 8 on your fingers. Lift bobbins 4 and 5 onto the backs of your thumbs, so that they sit above bobbins 1 and 8.

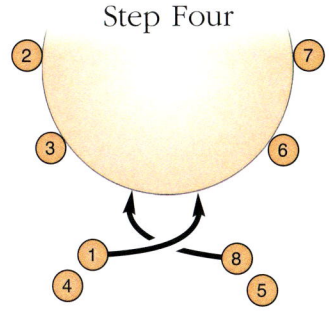
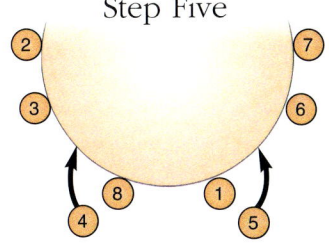
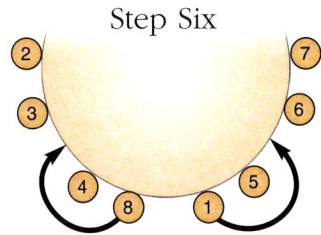

Step Four.
Bring bobbin 1 and 8 towards the centre. Use your fingers to cross bobbin 1 over bobbin 8 and drop them at the centre of the stand.

Step Five.
Drop bobbins 4 and 5 to the outside of bobbins 8 and 1.

Step Six.
Lift bobbins 8 and 1 and take them towards the outer edge, over bobbins 4 and 5. Drop bobbin 8, so that it is to the left of bobbin 4. Drop bobbin 1, so that it is to the right of bobbin 5.

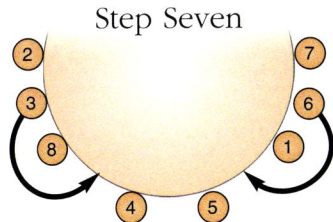

Step Seven.
Lift bobbins 3 and 6. Take them towards the centre over bobbins 8 and 1, and drop them next to bobbins 4 and 5.

Braid JC6

This 9-bobbin 'spot' braid is another popular pattern. It is usually used flat, either as a straight border or as a motif outline. It is worked in the same manner as JC1, except there is an extra bobbin that runs down the centre of the braid, parallel to the outer edges. This central bobbin is worked in a new way, which is illustrated in Figs 94 to 97. The full sequence of moves is shown in step-by-step diagrams on the following pages. The braid is built up in two alternate rows of movements, which are identical except for the treatment of bobbin 5. (Don't forget that the bobbins are renumbered at the end of each row). The spot pattern is created by having bobbin 5 in a contrasting colour to all the others.

Fig. 93.
Detail from a Miao collar. It shows an example of braid JC6 forming a border around an appliquéd and embroidered motif.
Courtesy of Gina Corrigan

JC6 Summary.

First Row
The outermost bobbins go under one, over one, under one, then cross (right over left) over the central bobbin.

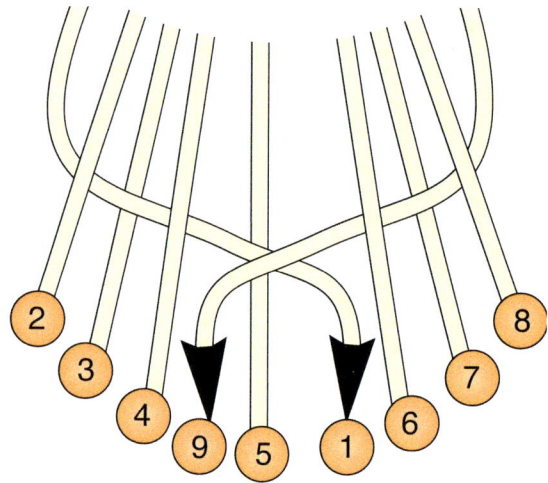

Second Row
The outermost bobbins go under one, over one, under one, then cross (right over left) under the central bobbin.

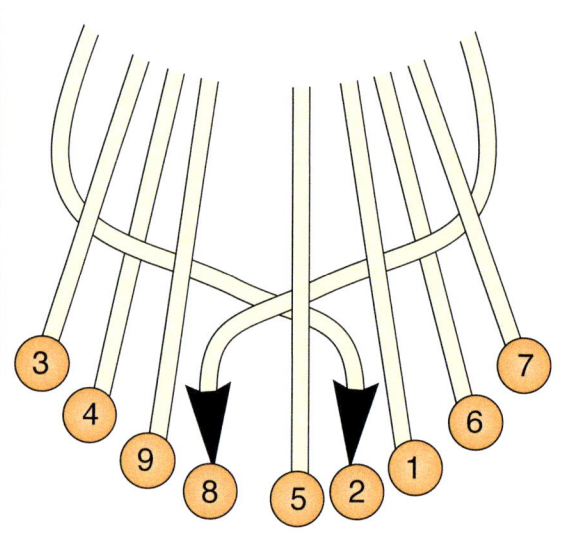

Braiding

The following photographs illustrate just the new moves found in this braid.

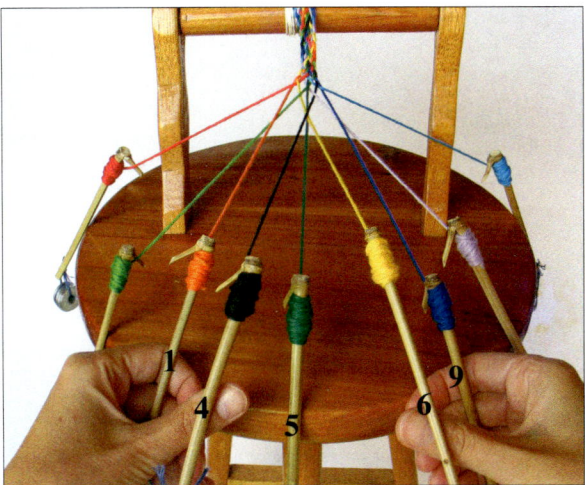

Fig. 94.
This corresponds to Step Three of the Second Row. At the centre of the stand, the bobbins are lifted in the usual way, with bobbins 1 and 9 on the fingers, and bobbins 4 and 6 lifted on the backs of the thumbs.

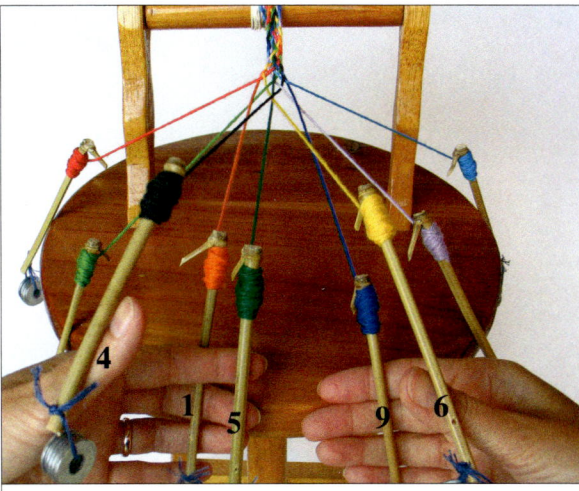

Fig. 95.
This corresponds to Step Four of the Second Row. Now bring your lefthand index finger over bobbin 1, and use it to lift bobbin 5. Bring bobbin 5 up so that is sits above bobbin 1 but below bobbin 4.

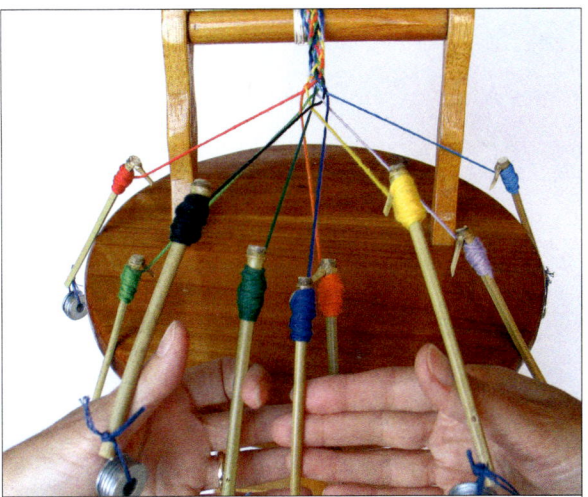

Fig. 96.
This corresponds to Step Five of the Second Row. Continue lifting all the bobbins and cross bobbin 9 over 1.

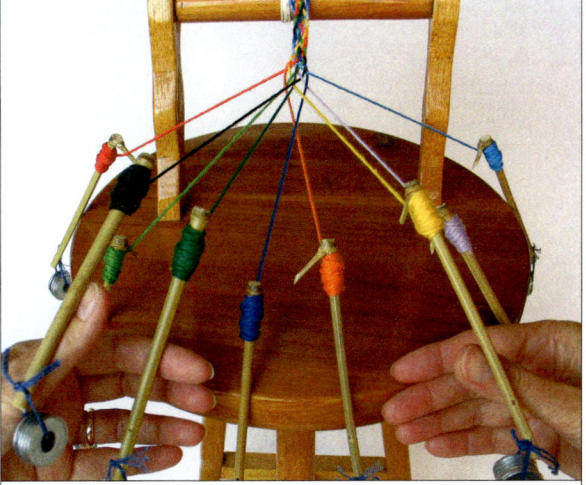

Fig. 97.
This also corresponds to Step Five of the Second Row. Drop bobbins 9 and 1 at the centre of the stand.

Braiding

First Row.

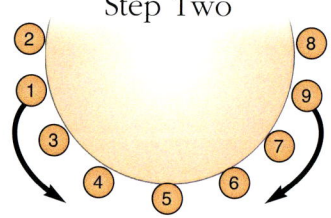
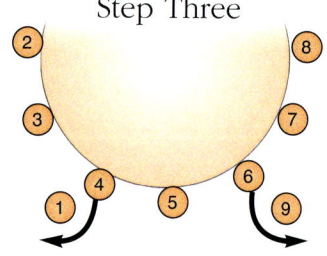

Step One.
Pick up bobbins 2 and 8, and move them away from the centre, over bobbins 1 and 9. Drop bobbins 2 and 8 so that they are on the outside edges.

Step Two.
Lift bobbins 1 and 9, and bring them towards the centre, over bobbins 3 and 7.

Step Three.
Continue lifting bobbins 1 and 9 on your fingers. Lift bobbins 4 and 6 onto the backs of your thumbs, so that they sit above bobbins 1 and 9.

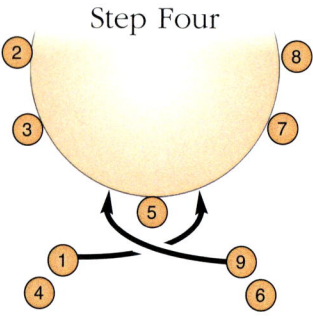
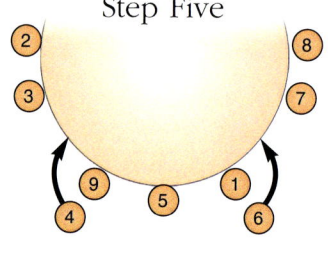

Step Four.
Bring bobbin 1 and 9 towards the centre. Use your fingers to cross bobbin 9 over bobbin 1. Drop bobbins 9 and 1 so that they sit either side of bobbin 5.

Step Five.
Drop bobbins 4 and 6 to the outside of bobbins 9 and 1.

Mentally renumber the bobbins before starting the second row.

Braiding

Second Row.

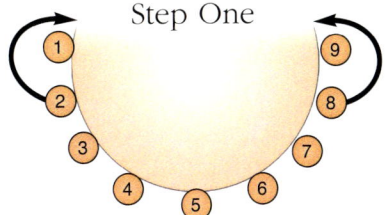
Step One

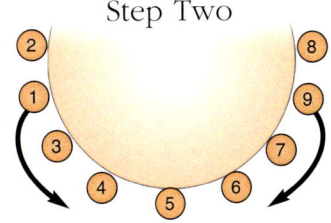
Step Two

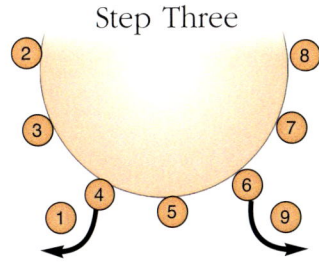
Step Three

Step One.
Pick up bobbins 2 and 8, and move them away from the centre, over bobbins 1 and 9. Drop bobbins 2 and 8 so that they are on the outside edges.

Step Two.
Lift bobbins 1 and 9, and bring them towards the centre, over bobbins 3 and 7.

Step Three.
Continue lifting bobbins 1 and 9 on your fingers. Lift bobbins 4 and 6 onto the backs of your thumbs, so that they sit above bobbins 1 and 9.

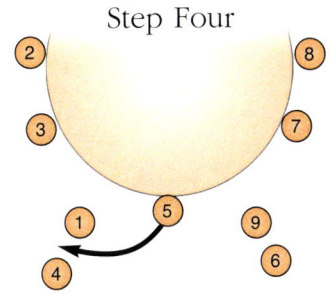
Step Four

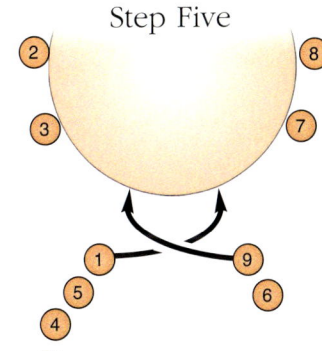
Step Five

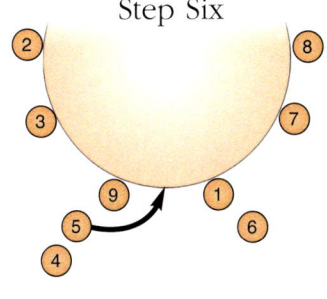
Step Six

Step Four.
Continue lifting all four bobbins. Bring the left-hand index finger to the front of bobbin 1 and use it to lift up bobbin 5, so that it sits above bobbin 1 but below bobbin 4.

Step Five.
Lift bobbins 4, 5 and 6 so that bobbins 1 and 9 can be brought together underneath them. Use your fingers to cross bobbin 9 over bobbin 1. Drop bobbins 9 and 1 so that they sit at the centre of the stand.

Step Six.
Drop bobbin 5 so that it sits between bobbins 9 and 1.

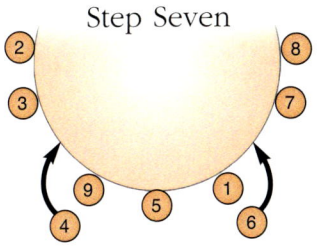
Step Seven

Step Seven.
Drop bobbins 4 and 6 so that they sit to the outside of bobbins 9 and 1.

You are now ready to repeat the first row starting with Step One.

Braid JC7

Some samples highlight the spot design of JC6 by having the central thread slightly thicker than the others. Another way of enhancing the spot is to alter the number of repeats of each row so that the upper float is extended. Here the sequence of movements must be altered so that either the first and/or the second row are repeated. Although it is possible to repeat a row more than twice, examples of this have yet to be found (except as an error). Working a sequence of {first row, first row, second row, second row} will extend not only the spot but the space between them. The examples shown in Fig. 98 are the more common sequence of {first row, first row, second row}. This elongates the spot to the back of the braid. When the braid is finished, it will need turning over so that the longer spot is on the surface. Braiding the long spot on the surface {first row, second row, second row} produces the same effect but requires more effort.

Fig. 98.
A Miao panel, with detail, showing a border of tiny braids less than 2 mm wide. The 'spot' pattern has been emphasised by repeating one of the rows in the braiding sequence, and is an example of JC7.
Courtesy of Deanie Neubofer.

JC7 Summary.

Work JC6 but repeat the following sequence:

First Row - The outermost bobbins go under one, over one, under one, then cross (right over left) over the central bobbin.

First Row - The outermost bobbins go under one, over one, under one, then cross (right over left) over the central bobbin.

Second Row - The outermost bobbins go under one, over one, under one, then cross (right over left) under the central bobbin.

Braid JC8

This is a different pattern created on the same structure as JC6, so the movements remain the same. The green and black chevrons, with a white spot, is a popular design in an area near Taijiang. Arrange the colours so that bobbins 1, 3, 7, 9 are black, bobbins 2, 4, 6, 8 are green and bobbin 5 is white.

JC8 Summary.

First Row
The outermost bobbins go under one, over one, under one, then cross (right over left) over the central bobbin.

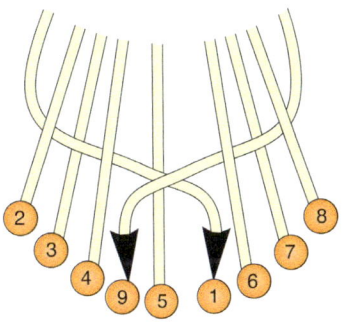

Second Row
The outermost bobbins go under one, over one, under one, then cross (right over left) under the central bobbin.

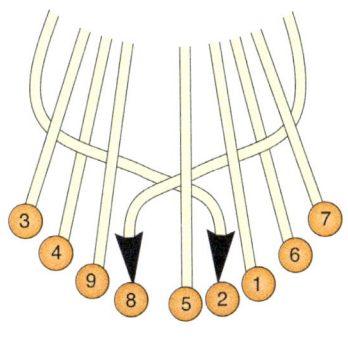

Fig. 99.
This tiny panel measures just 8 cm by 4.5 cm. It is from the back of the neck on a Miao festival jacket. In spite of its size, it is covered in fine handiwork, including cross-stitch, folded silk appliqué, and silk braids JC8 bordered with striped braids JC4.

Braiding

Fig. 100 (above).
A Miao sleeve panel with outlines created from braid JC6. The motifs are made from pleated braid JC1.
Courtesy of Gina Corrigan.

Fig. 101 (below).
Detail from the Bai collar shown in Fig. 102. The green and yellow braid is an example of braid JC9. The pink and white is slightly different. Both braids are approximately 2 mm wide.
Courtesy of Martin Conlan.

Braid JC9

This 11-bobbin braid is the most complex structure shown in this book, so it is best attempted when you are familiar with the other braids. Three bobbins run parallel to the edge of the braid, whilst the others work alternating sequences. The braid is made of four different rows that repeat to form the final pattern (don't forget that the bobbins are renumbered after every row). The example shown in Fig. 101 has yellow silk starting on bobbins 5, 6 and 7, whilst the rest are green.

JC9 Summary.

First Row
The outermost bobbins go under one, over one, under one and over one. They then cross (left over right) over the central bobbin, and continue outwards over one.

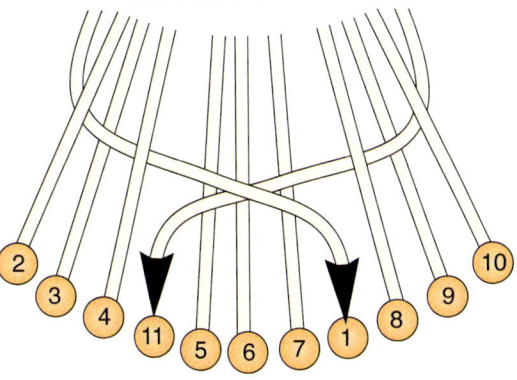

Second Row
The outermost bobbins go under one and over three. They then cross (left over right) under the central bobbin, and continue outwards under one.

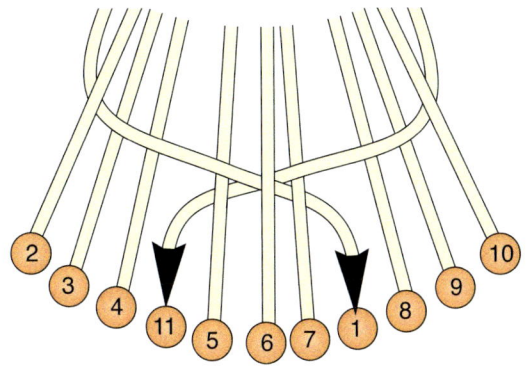

Third Row
The outermost bobbins go under one, over one, and under two. They then cross (left over right) over the central bobbin, and continue outwards under one.

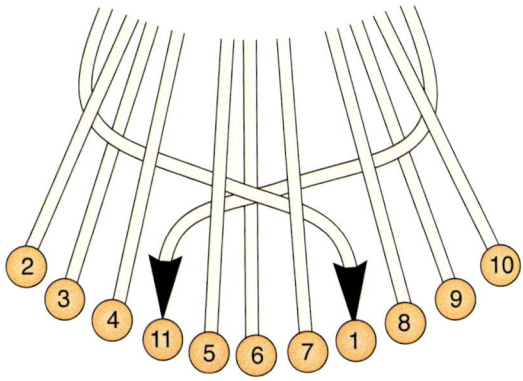

Fourth Row
The outermost bobbins go under one, over two and under one. They then cross (left over right) under the central bobbin, and continue outwards over one.

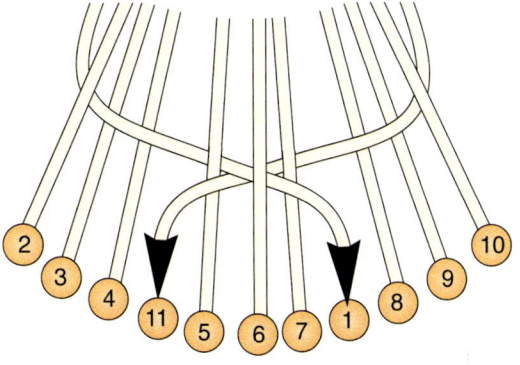

Braiding

Fig. 102.
A Bai collar from Yunnan Province measuring approximately 32 cm by 4 cm. The detail (Fig. 101) shows the precise embroidery and an example of braid JC9.
Courtesy of Martin Conlan.

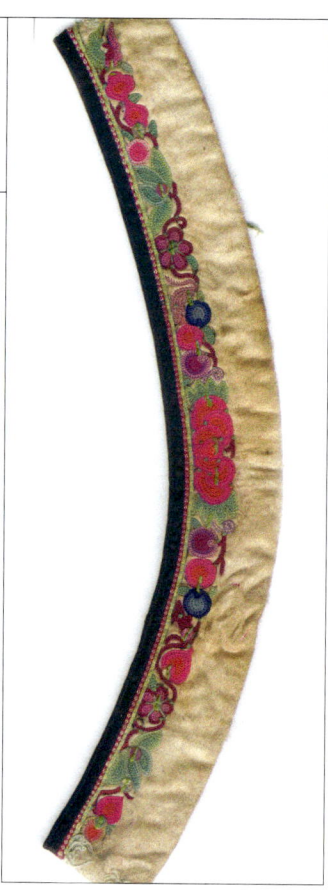

First Row.

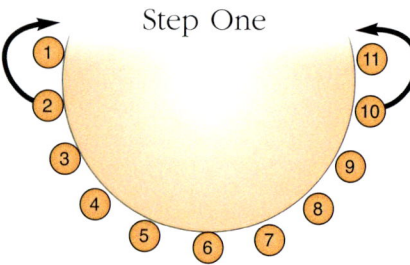

Step One.
Pick up bobbins 2 and 10 and move them away from the centre, over bobbins 1 and 11. Drop bobbins 2 and 10 so that they are on the outside edges.

Step Two.
Lift bobbins 1 and 11 and take them towards the centre, going over one bobbin each. Drop bobbin 1 between bobbin 3 and 4. Drop bobbin 11 between bobbin 8 and 9.

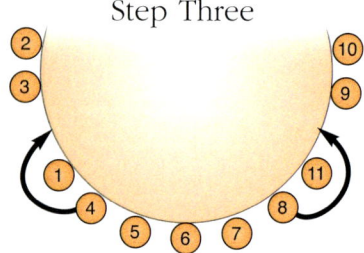

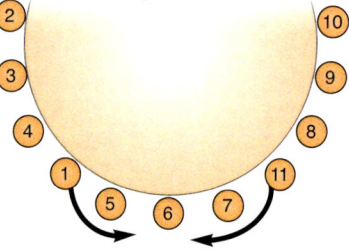

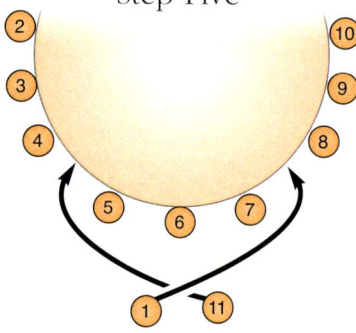

Step Three.
Lift bobbins 4 and 8 and take them away from the centre, going over one bobbin each. Drop bobbin 4 between bobbin 3 and 1. Drop bobbin 8 between bobbin 11 and 9.

Step Four.
Lift bobbin 1 and 11 towards the centre, going over bobbins 5 and 7.

Step Five.
Cross bobbin 1 over bobbin 11, over the top of bobbin 6. Continue taking them towards the outer edges, going over bobbins 5 and 7. Place them down so that bobbin 11 sits between 4 and 5, and bobbin 1 sits between 7 and 8.

Braiding

Second Row.

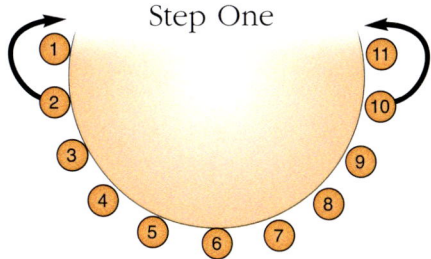
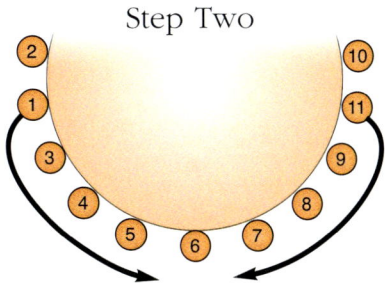
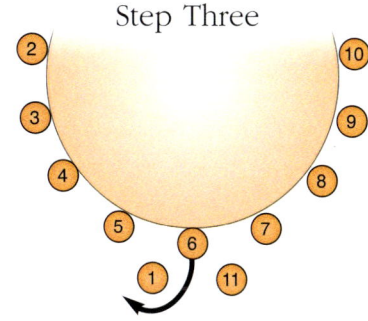

Step One.
Pick up bobbins 2 and 10 and move them away from the centre, over bobbins 1 and 11. Drop bobbins 2 and 10 so that they are on the outside edges.

Step Two.
Lift bobbins 1 and 11 and take them towards the centre, going over three bobbins each.

Step Three.
Continue lifting bobbin 1 and 11 on the fingers. Pick up bobbin 6 on the back of your thumb.

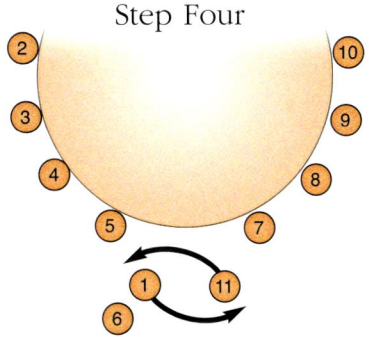
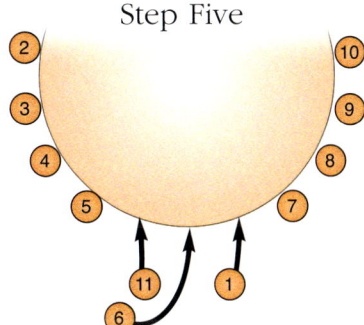
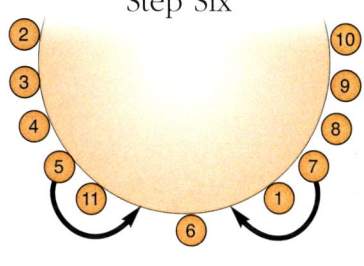

Step Four.
Cross bobbin 1 over 11, underneath bobbin 6.

Step Five.
Drop bobbin 6 down in the centre of the stand. Drop bobbins 11 and 1 either side of bobbin 6.

Step Six.
Lift bobbins 5 and 7 and move them towards the centre, going over one bobbin each. Drop them so that they sit either side of bobbin 6.

Braiding

Third Row.

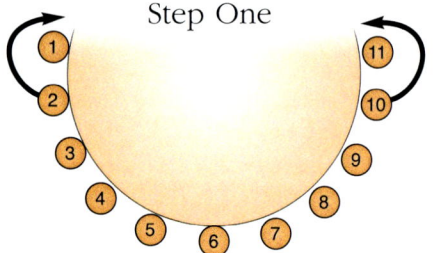

Step One.
Pick up bobbins 2 and 10 and move them away from the centre, over bobbins 1 and 11. Drop bobbins 2 and 10 so that they are on the outside edges.

Step Two.
Lift bobbins 1 and 11 and take them towards the centre, going over one bobbin each. Drop bobbin 1 between bobbin 3 and 4. Drop bobbin 11 between bobbin 8 and 9.

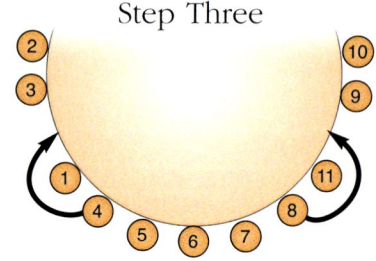

Step Three.
Lift bobbins 4 and 8 and take them away from the centre, going over one bobbin each. Drop bobbin 4 between bobbin 3 and 1. Drop bobbin 8 between bobbin 11 and 9.

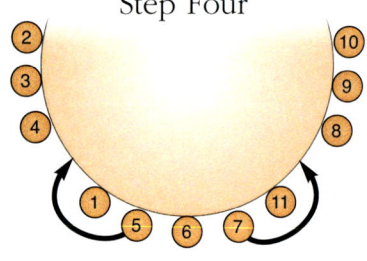

Step Four.
Lift bobbins 5 and 7 and take them away from the centre, going over one bobbin each. Drop bobbin 5 between bobbin 4 and 1. Drop bobbin 7 between bobbin 11 and 8.

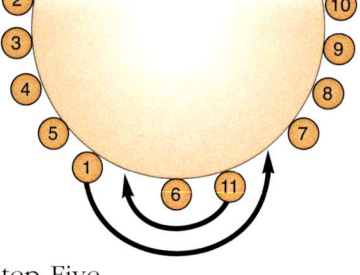

Step Five.
Lift bobbins 1 and 11. Drop bobbin 11 to the left of bobbin 6, and drop bobbin 1 to the right of bobbin 6.

Step Six.
Lift bobbins 5 and 7 and take them towards the centre over one bobbin each. Drop bobbin 5 between bobbins 11 and 6. Drop bobbin 7 between bobbins 6 and 1.

Braiding

Fourth Row.

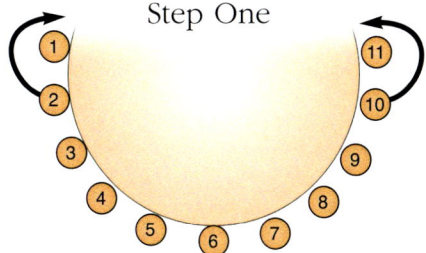

Step One.
Pick up bobbins 2 and 10 and move them away from the centre, over bobbins 1 and 11. Drop bobbins 2 and 10 so that they are on the outside edges.

Step Two.
Lift bobbins 1 and 11 and take them towards the centre, going over two bobbins each. Drop bobbin 1 between bobbins 4 and 5. Drop bobbin 11 between bobbins 7 and 8.

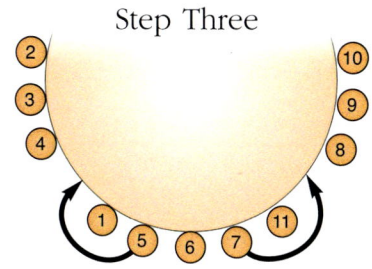

Step Three.
Lift bobbins 5 and 7 and take them away from the centre going over one bobbin each. Drop bobbin 5 between bobbins 4 and 1. Drop bobbin 7 between bobbins 11 and 8.

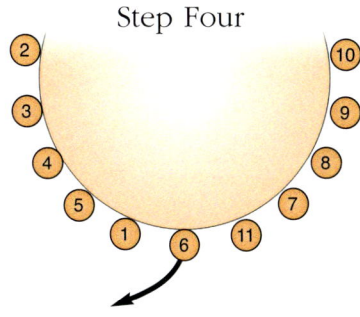

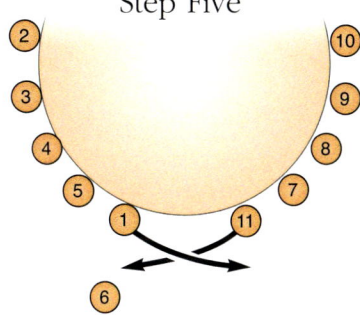

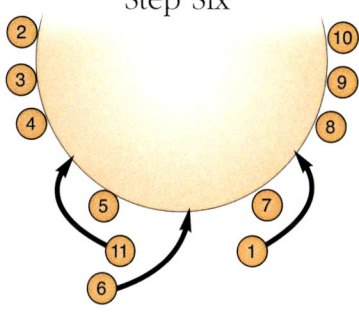

Step Four.
Lift bobbin 6 onto the back of your left-hand thumb.

Step Five.
Lift bobbins 1 and 11 and cross them over each other (1 over 11).

Step Six.
Drop bobbin 6 onto the centre of the stand. Continue taking bobbins 1 and 11 towards the outer edges, going over bobbins 5 and 7. Place them down so that 11 sits between 4 and 5, and 1 sits between 7 and 8.

Braiding

Fig. 103.
A Dong Hat covered with decorative features including braid embroidery. A detail from the hat can be seen in Fig. 75.
Courtesy of Elizabeth Andrews.

Braid JC10

This 12-bobbin braid is worked in two colours. Every sixth row there is a slightly different set of moves. This creates a subtle scallop-edged effect. This helps to smooth the circular pattern that is produced with the two colours. The example shown in Fig 104 starts with bobbins 5, 6, 7 and 8 wound with white silk, whilst the rest are wound with purple.

Fig. 104.
A Sani hat from near Kunming, Yunnan Province. The decoration includes a purple and white version of braid JC10.
Courtesy of Gina Corrigan.

JC10 Summary.

First to Fifth Row
The outermost bobbins go under one, over one, under one, over one, under one, then cross in the centre (right over left).

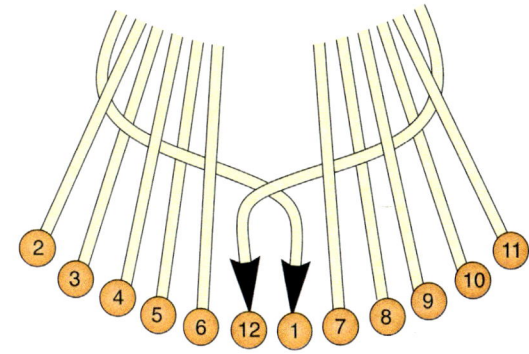

Sixth Row
The outermost bobbins go over two, under one, over one, under one, then cross in the centre (right over left).

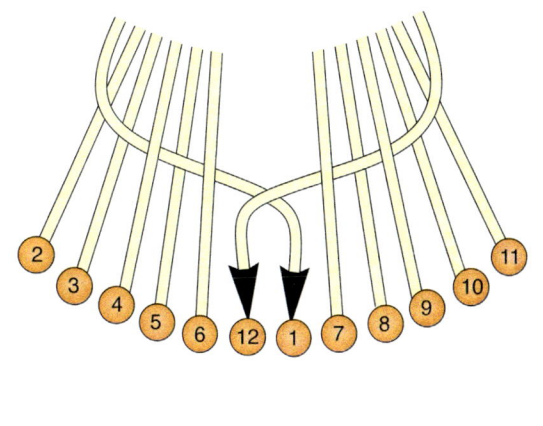

Braiding

First to Fifth Row.

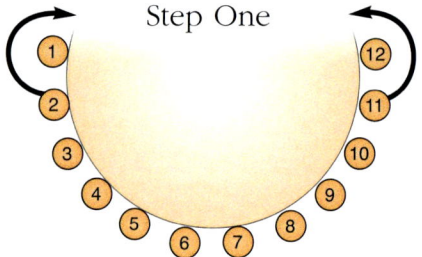

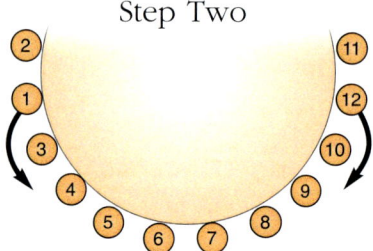

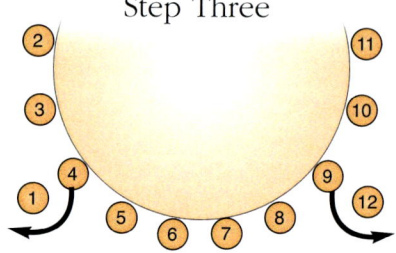

Step One.
Pick up bobbins 2 and 11 and move them away from the centre, over bobbins 1 and 12. Drop bobbins 2 and 11 so that they are on the outside edges.

Step Two.
Lift bobbins 1 and 12 and take them towards the centre so that they go over bobbins 3 and 10

Step Three.
Hold bobbins 1 and 12 in the lower three fingers of each hand and bring the index finger and thumb above these bobbins. Lift bobbins 4 and 9 onto the back of the thumbs, so that they sit above bobbins 1 and 12.

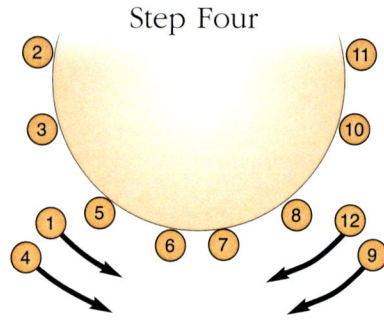

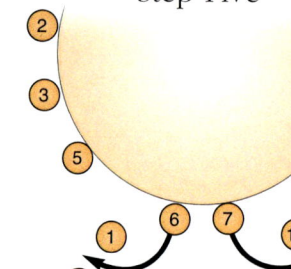

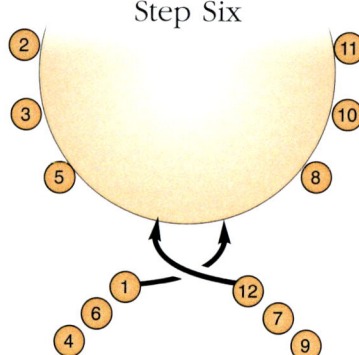

Step Four.
Continue lifting all four bobbins and take them towards the centre over bobbins 5 and 8.

Step Five.
Continue lifting all four bobbins and pick up bobbin 6 and 7 on the index fingers, so that they sit above bobbins 1 and 12, but below bobbins 4 and 9.

Step Six.
Cross bobbin 12 over bobbin 1 and drop them at the centre of the stand.

Braiding

Sixth Row.

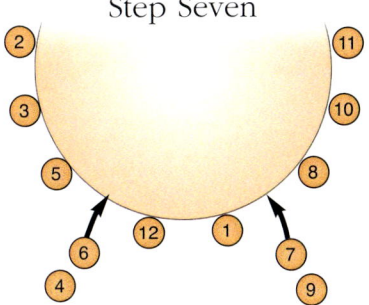

Step Seven

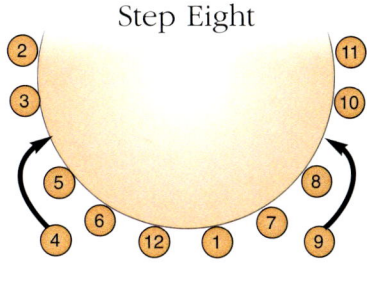

Step Eight

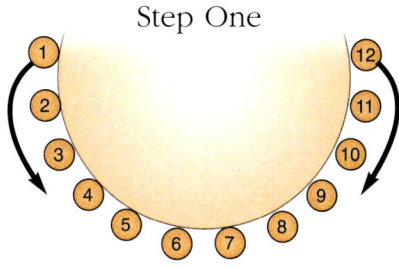

Step One

Step Seven.
Drop bobbins 6 and 7 either side of bobbins 12 and 1.

Step Eight.
Take bobbins 4 and 9 back towards the edge and drop them back in their original positions so that bobbin 4 sits between 3 and 5, and bobbin 9 sits between bobbin 8 and 10.

Step One.
Lift bobbins 1 and 12 and take them towards the centre so that they both go over two bobbins each.

Omit Step Two, then repeat Steps Three to Eight of the First Row, before starting the whole sequence again.

Fig. 105.
A close-up showing acrylic braids adorning a shoulder bag made for the tourist market. The blue, pink and white version of braid JC10 is approximately 5 mm wide. This 3-colour version started with bobbins 1, 2, 11 and 12 in blue, bobbins 3, 4, 9 and 10 in pink, and bobbins 5, 6, 7 and 8 in white.
Courtesy of Deanie Neubofer.

Braid JC11

This is a 12-bobbin braid, two of which interlink at intervals along the outer edge, whilst the others form a 6-ridge braid. The working sequence is repeated after every three rows. The decorative edge is highlighted by starting with bobbins 1 and 12 in a different colour from the rest.

Fig. 106.
A Miao lady, from Baduo village, near Duyun, Guizhou Province, making braid with bamboo bobbins weighted with ceramic shapes. The detail (right) shows a close up of the braid, which is made from synthetic yarns.
Courtesy of Ien Rappoldt.

JC11 Summary.

First row
The outermost bobbins go under and back over the second outermost bobbins. The second outermost bobbins work towards the centre going over two, under one, over one, then cross in the centre (left over right).

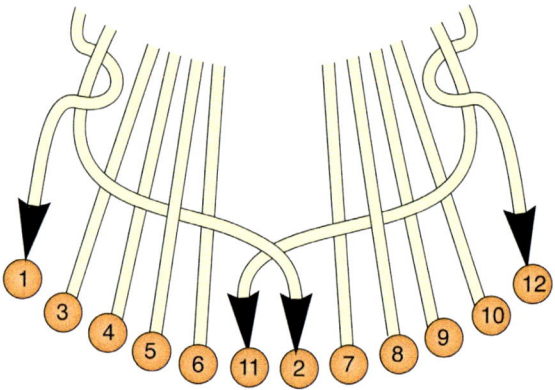

Second and third row
The second outermost bobbins go over two, under one, over one, then cross in the centre (left over right).

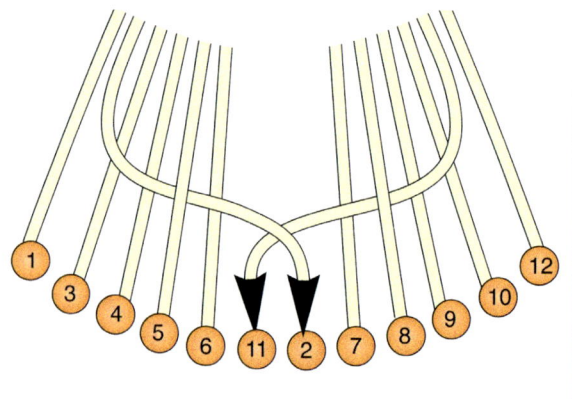

— 88 —

Braiding

First Row.

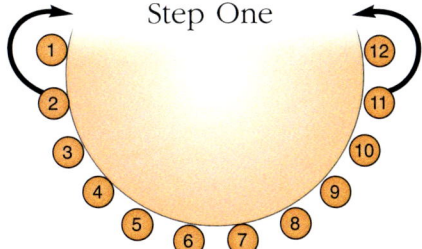
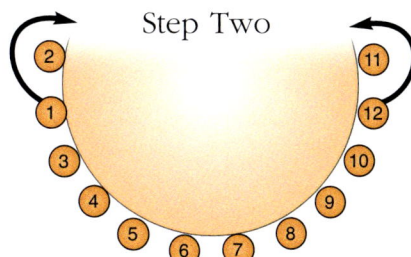
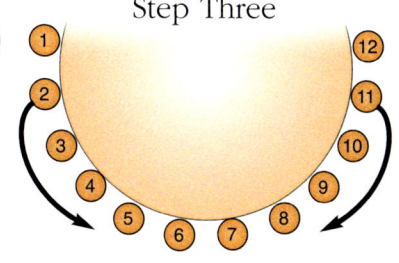

Step One.
Pick up bobbins 2 and 11 and move them away from the centre, over bobbins 1 and 12. Drop bobbins 2 and 11 so that they are on the outside edges.

Step Two.
Lift up bobbins 1 and 12 and move them away from the centre, over bobbins 2 and 11. Drop bobbins 1 and 12 so that they are back on the outside edges.

Step Three.
Lift bobbins 2 and 11 and take them towards the centre so that they both go over two bobbins (Bobbin 2 will go over 3 and 4, whilst bobbin 11 will go over 10 and 9)

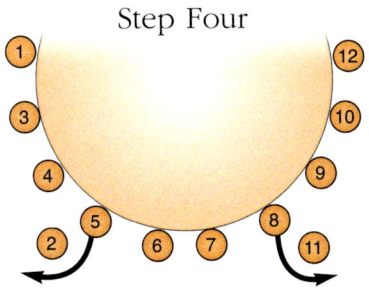
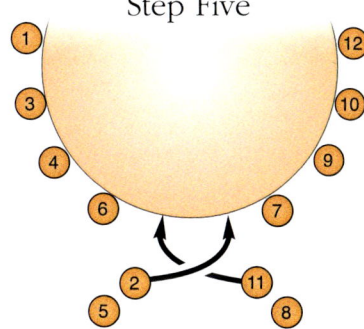
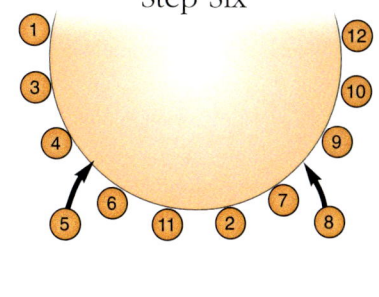

Step Four.
Continue lifting bobbins 2 and 11 with the fingers and pick up bobbins 5 and 8 on the backs of your thumbs, so that they are above bobbins 2 and 11.

Step Five.
Continue lifting all four bobbins and take them towards the centre, going over bobbins 6 and 7. Cross bobbin 2 over 11 and drop them both at the centre of the stand.

Step Six.
Drop bobbins 5 and 8 either side of bobbins 6 and 7 (so that bobbin 5 is between bobbin 4 and 6, and bobbin 8 is between 7 and 9).

Second and Third Row.

Omit Step One and Step Two. Work Step Three to Six of the First Row.

Braid JC12

This 12-bobbin braid is made from six bobbins that obliquely interlace from side to side, whilst the other six work parallel to the edge of the braid. The sequence of moves follows a two row repeat. The braid is worked in three colours, creating a pattern of alternating blocks edged with two lines of colour. Bobbins 4, 6 and 8 form one block of colour, whilst the bobbins 5, 7 and 9 form the other. The rest of the bobbins need to be in a third colour to make the edges.

JC12 Summary.

First row
The outermost bobbins go under one and over one, then cross (left over right) between the central bobbins with the even ones lifted.

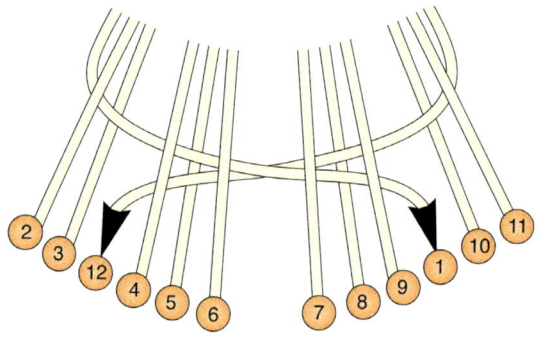

Second row
The outermost bobbins go under one and over one, then cross (left over right) between the central bobbins with the odd ones lifted.

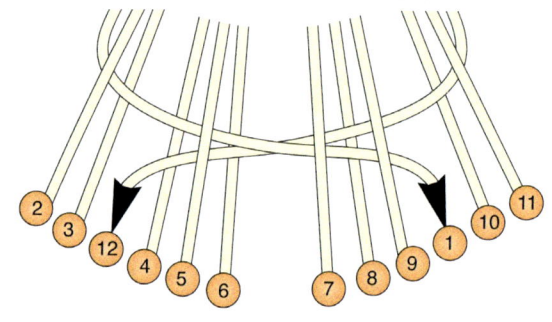

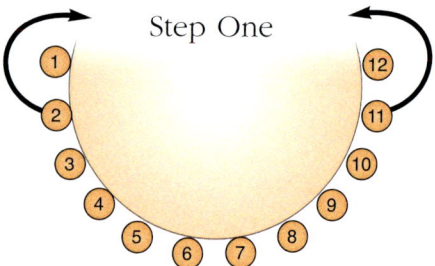

Step One.
Pick up bobbins 2 and 11 and move them away from the centre, over bobbins 1 and 12. Drop bobbins 2 and 11 so that they are on the outside edges.

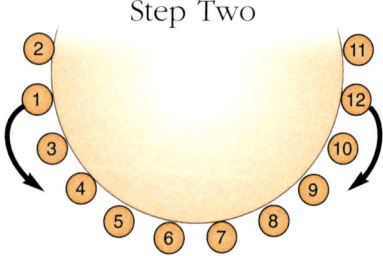

Step Two.
Lift bobbins 1 and 12 and take them towards the centre, going over bobbins 3 and 10.

Fig. 107.
Another Sani hat from near Kunming, Yunnan Province. The lower braid is a version of JC12, made using 3-ply threads. *Courtesy of Gina Corrigan.*

Braiding

First Row.

Step One and Two then...

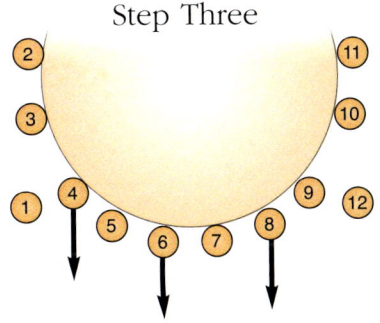 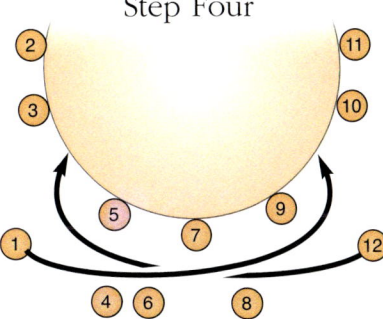 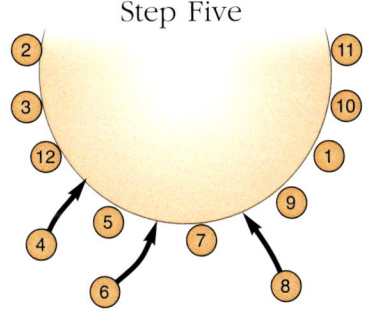

Step Three.
Continue lift bobbins 1 and 12 in the lower fingers. Pick up bobbin 4 and 6 between the left-hand index finger and thumb, and bobbin 8 between the right-hand index finger and thumb.

Step Four.
Bring bobbin 1 and 12 towards the centre, under bobbins 4, 6 and 8. Cross bobbin 1 over bobbin 12. Drop bobbin 1 to the right of bobbin 9 and bobbin 12 to the left of bobbin 5.

Step Five.
Place bobbins 4, 6 and 8 back to their original positions next to bobbins 5, 7 and 9.

Second Row.

Step One and Two then...

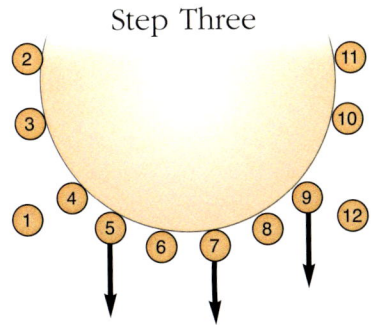 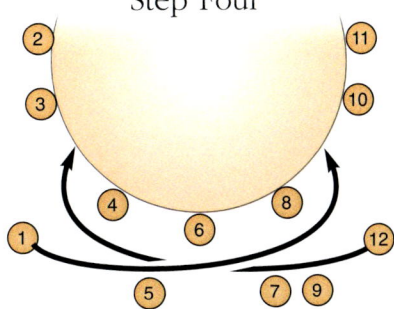 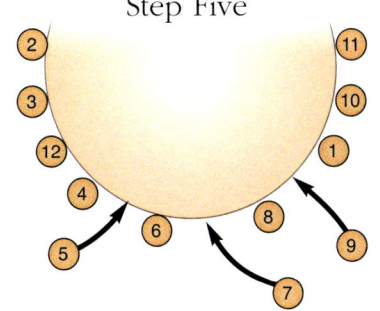

Step Three.
Continue lift bobbins 1 and 12 in the lower fingers. Pick up bobbin 5 between the left-hand index finger and thumb, and bobbins 7 and 9 between the right-hand index finger and thumb.

Step Four.
Bring bobbin 1 and 12 towards the centre, under bobbins 5, 7 and 9. Cross bobbin 1 over bobbin 12. Drop bobbin 1 to the right of bobbin 8 and bobbin 12 to the left of bobbin 4.

Step Five.
Place bobbins 5, 7 and 9 back to their original positions next to bobbins 4, 6 and 8

Braid JC13

This 12-bobbin braid is a wider version of braid JC4. The resulting braid consists of two interlinked 6-bobbin, 5-ridge braids. The two halves are usually worked in different colours creating the distinctive stripe pattern. This wider version of stripe makes a striking border. It is also used for making the overlaid loops (see page 124). Starts with bobbins 1 to 6 wound with a different colour to bobbins 7 to 12.

JC13 Summary.

The outermost bobbins go under one, over one, under one, over one, under one, then cross twice in the centre (right over left).

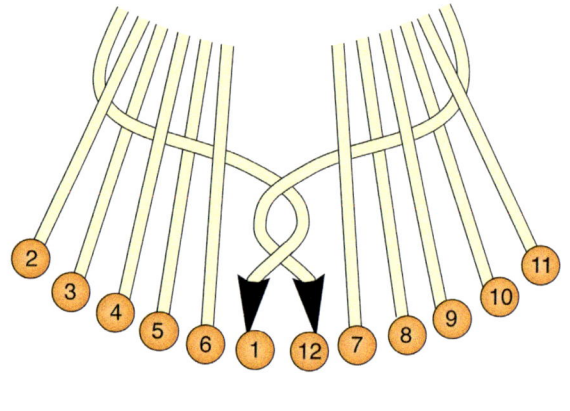

Fig. 108.
A detail of the Dong baby carrier seen in Fig. 109. The two-tone green striped braid is an example of braid JC13. It has been applied as a straight flat border and a 'looped' border design.
Courtesy of Martin Conlan.

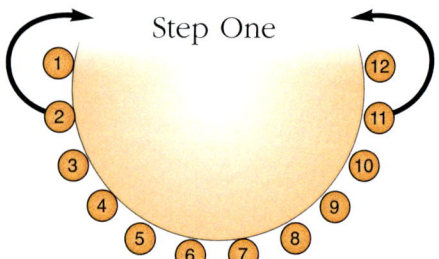

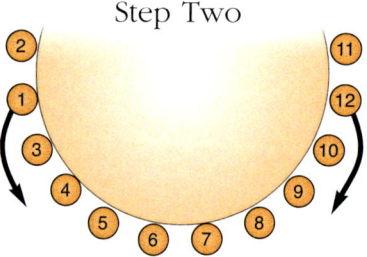

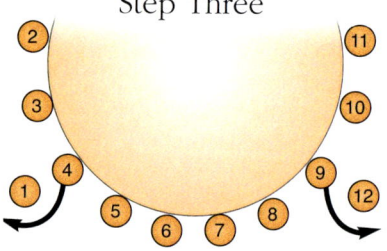

Step One.
Pick up bobbins 2 and 11 and move them away from the centre, over bobbins 1 and 12. Drop bobbins 2 and 11 so that they are on the outside edges.

Step Two.
Lift bobbins 1 and 12, and bring them towards the centre, over bobbins 3 and 10.

Step Three.
Continue lifting bobbins 1 and 12 on your lower three fingers, with the index finger and thumb above the bobbins. Pick up bobbins 4 and 9 onto the backs of your thumbs, so that they are above bobbins 1 and 12.

Braiding

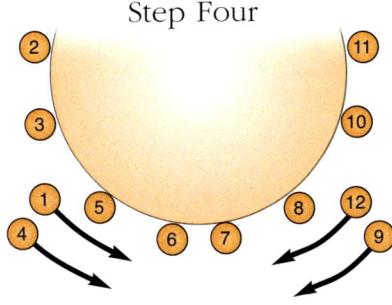

Step Four.
Continue lifting all four bobbins towards the centre, over bobbins 5 and 8.

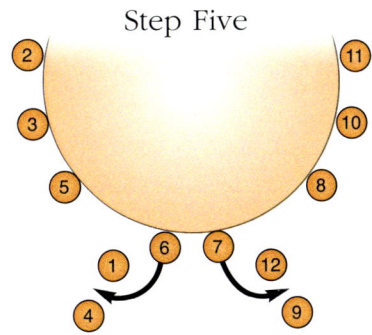

Step Five.
Lift bobbins 6 and 7 on your index fingers, so that they are above bobbins 1 and 12, but below bobbins 4 and 9.

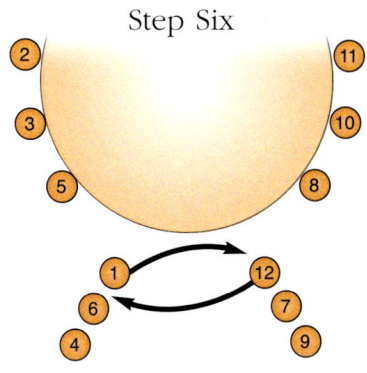

Step Six.
Bring bobbins 1 and 12 under the other four and cross bobbin 12 over 1.

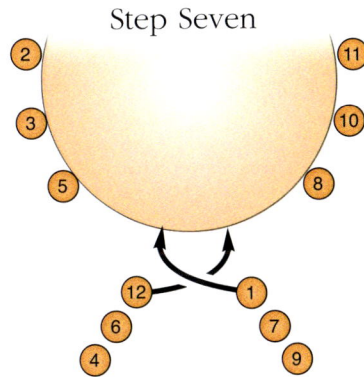

Step Seven.
Cross bobbin 1 over 12 and drop them both down at the centre of the stand.

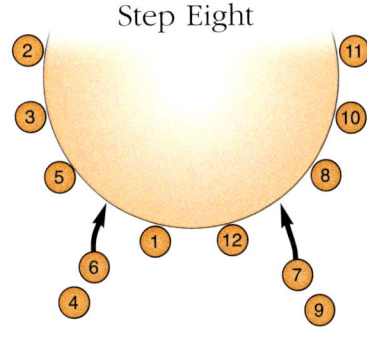

Step Eight:
Drop bobbins 6 and 7 to the outside of bobbins 1 and 12.

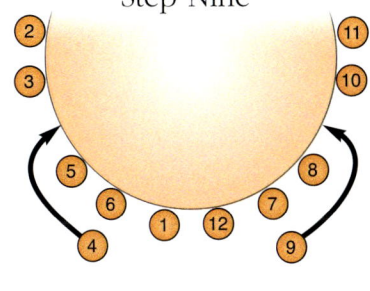

Step Nine.
Move bobbins 4 and 9 away from the centre and drop them into their original positions so that they sit between 3 and 5, and 8 and 10 respectively.

Braiding

Braid JC14

This one-colour, 15-bobbin braid is often used by the Dong people. The structure is plain oblique interlacing, which makes it very flat and wide. It is used flat, but it is more often found making the triangular coiling (see page 122). The summary seems straight forward, but the Dong work this swiftly by holding many bobbins in their hands. These step-by-step details are shown overleaf.

Fig. 109 (opposite page).
Baby carriers of this type are worn strapped on the back with ties taken over the shoulders, across the chest and back around the waist. They are often highly decorated, like this Dong one that measures approximately 33 cm by 47 cm.
Courtesy of Martin Conlan.

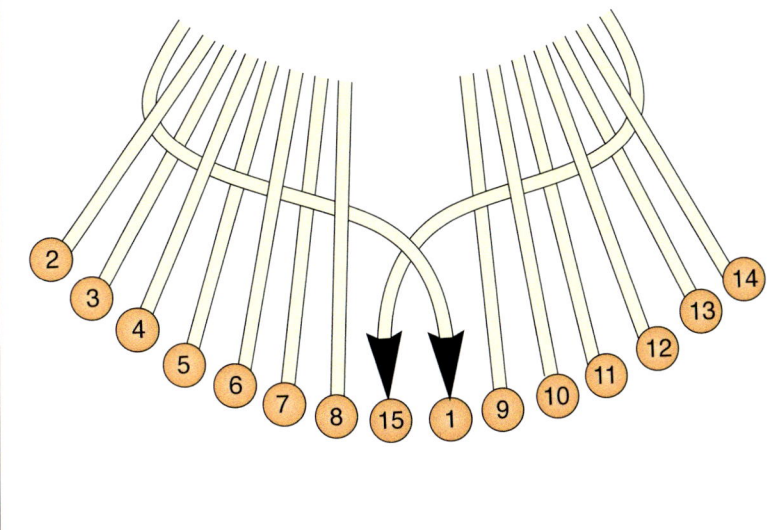

JC14 Summary.

The outermost bobbins go under one, over one, under one, over one, under one and over one. Then the left-hand bobbin only goes under one and over one.

Fig. 110 (below).
This detail from Fig 109, shows three S-shaped motifs that have been made with braid JC14. The triangular coiling is described on page 122.
Courtesy of Martin Conlan.

Braiding

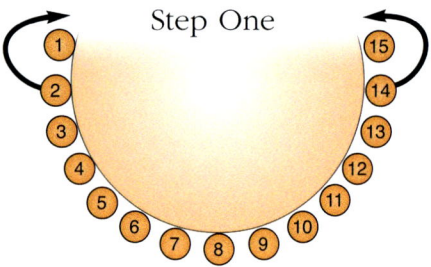

Step One.
Pick up bobbins 2 and 14 and move them away from the centre, over bobbins 1 and 15. Drop bobbins 2 and 14 so that they are on the outside edges.

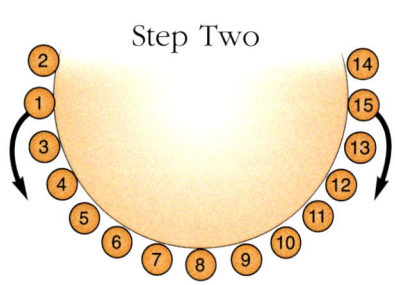

Step Two.
Lift bobbins 1 and 15 and take them towards the centre, going over bobbins 3 and 13. Hold bobbin 1 on the ring and little finger, and bobbin 15 on the lower three fingers.

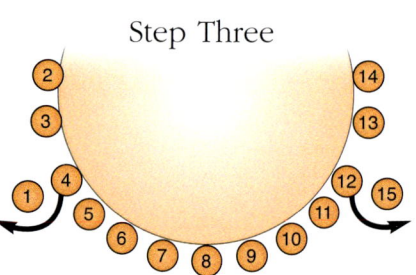

Step Three.
Continue lifting bobbin 1 and 15. Have the index fingers and thumbs above bobbins 1 and 15, and pick up bobbins 4 and 12 on the back of thumbs, so that they sit above bobbins 1 and 15.

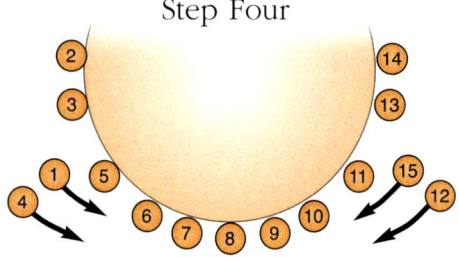

Step Four.
Move all four bobbins towards the centre, going over bobbins 5 and 11.

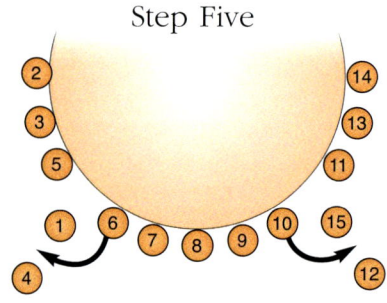

Step Five.
Lift bobbins 6 and 10 onto the index fingers, above bobbins 1 and 15, but below bobbins 4 and 12.

Braiding

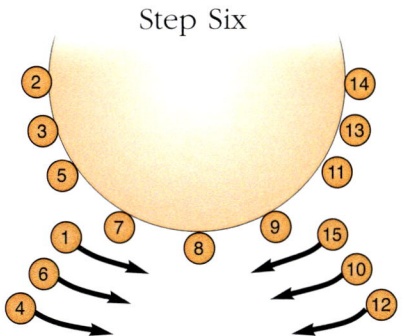

Step Six.
Bring all six bobbins towards the centre, going over 7 and 9.

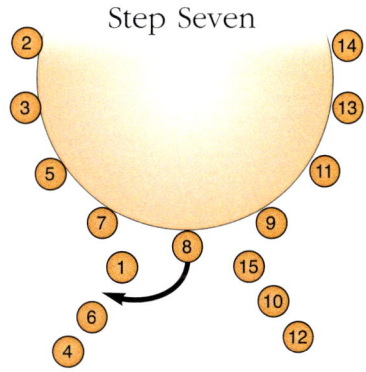

Step Seven.
With the tips of the middle fingers, lift bobbin 8 over bobbin 1 and onto the left-hand middle finger.

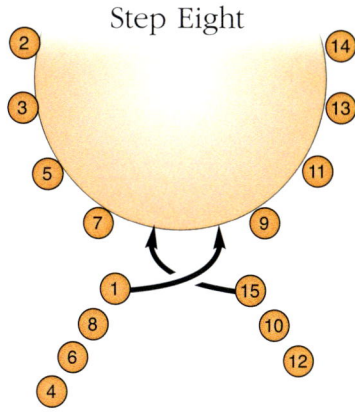

Step Eight.
Drop bobbin 15 down onto the centre of the stand, then drop bobbin 1 to the right-hand side of 15.

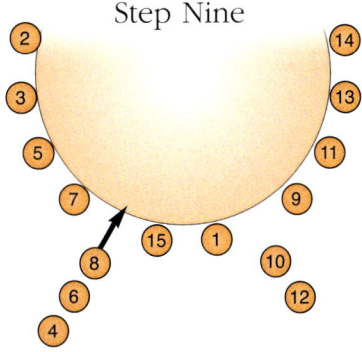

Step Nine.
Drop bobbin 8 to the left-hand side of bobbin 15

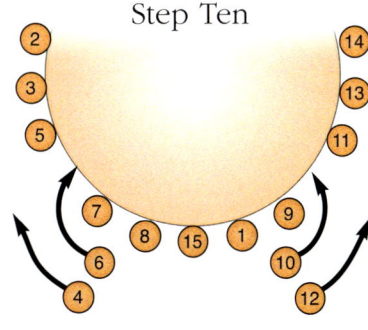

Step Ten.
Move all four remaining bobbins towards the outer edge of the stand. Drop bobbin 6 between 5 and 7, and bobbin 10 between 9 and 11.

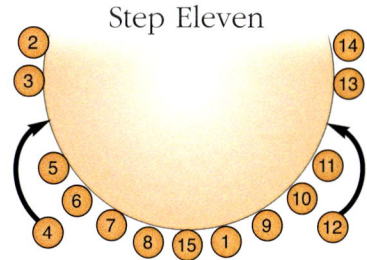

Step Eleven.
Drop bobbin 4 between 3 and 5, and bobbin 12 between 11 and 13.

Braid JC15

This is the same structure as JC14 so the sequence of moves remains the same. The zigzag pattern is created by starting with bobbins 1, 2 and 3 in one colour, whilst the others are in a different colour.

Fig. 111.
Another flat wide braid found on an old Dong hat. Three of these threads were once bright purple creating a zigzag pattern on the braid. The outer edges of the braids are held down with blanket stitch, whilst the inner edges are held with a row of running stitches.
Courtesy of Deanie Neuhofer.

JC15 & JC16 Summary.

The outermost bobbins go under one, over one, under one, over one, under one and over one.
Then the left-hand bobbin only goes under one and over one.

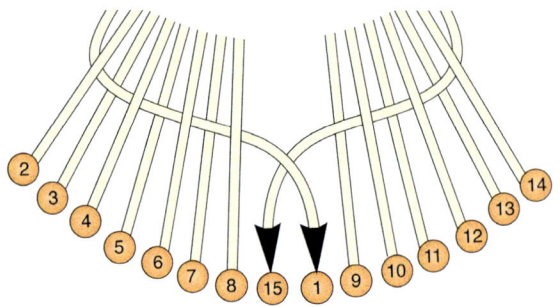

Braid JC16

This is the same structure as JC14 so the sequence of moves remains the same. This striking four colour pattern is created by starting with bobbins 1, 2, 3 and 4 in turquoise, bobbins 5, 6, 7 and 8 in purple, bobbins, 9, 10 and 11 in red, and bobbins 12, 13, 14 and 15 in yellow.

Fig. 112.
An example of braid JC16, found on a Miao panel from Pingzai, Liping County, Guizhou. This area is also home to many Dong people. The wide braid is applied with two rows of running stitch, one worked in turquoise silk and the other in orange.
Courtesy of Ien Rappoldt.

Braid JC17

This is a 15-bobbin braid made from three interlinked 5-bobbin braids. This popular structure can be found in many areas. The three stripes are highlighted by working with three different colours. The green, white and pink colour combination is typical of the Laohan braids. To achieve this pattern, start with bobbins 1 to 5 in green, bobbins 6 to 10 in white, and bobbins 11 to 15 in pink.

JC17 Summary.

The outermost bobbins go under one, over one, under one and over two. Then pick up the bobbins that are now to the outer side of bobbins just moved, and take them towards the centre going over two, then work just the left-hand one going under one and over one.

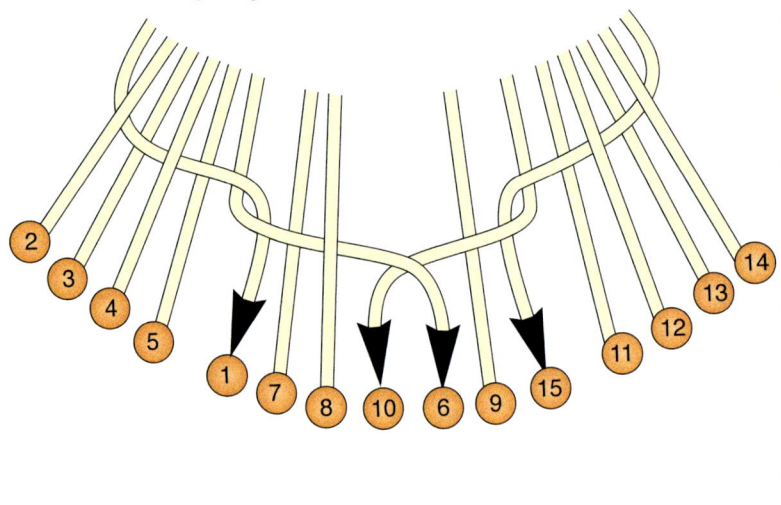

Fig. 113.
Detail of the shoe shown in Fig. 31. The combination of green, white and pink stripes is still popular with the Laohan people from Tianlong township, Pingba County, Guizhou.

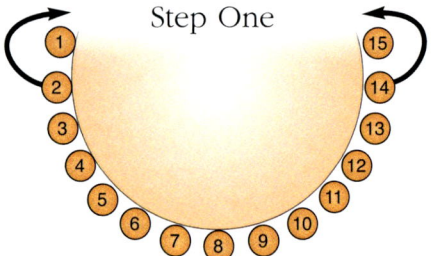

Step One.
Pick up bobbins 2 and 14 and move them away from the centre, over bobbins 1 and 15. Drop bobbins 2 and 14 so that they are on the outside edges.

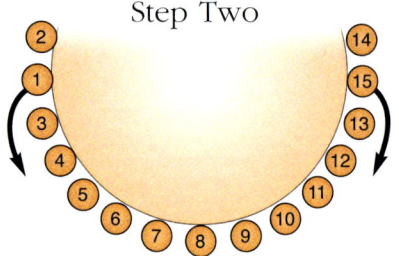

Step Two.
Lift bobbins 1 and 15 and take them towards the centre, going over bobbins 3 and 13.

Braiding

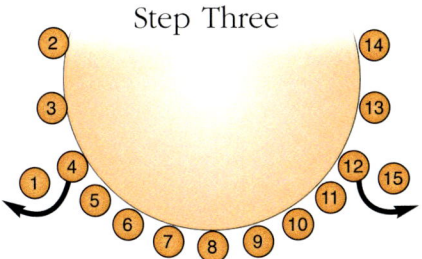

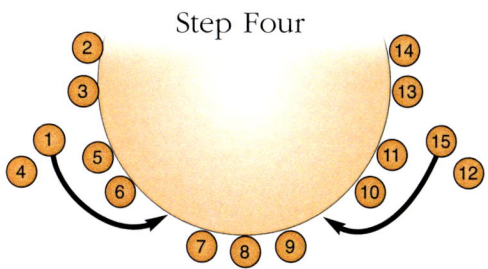

Step Three.
Continue lifting bobbins 1 and 15 on the lower fingers, and lift bobbins 4 and 12 onto the back of your thumbs, so that they are above bobbins 1 and 15.

Step Four.
Continue lifting all four bobbins towards the centre, going over two bobbins each. Drop bobbin 1 between bobbins 6 and 7. Drop bobbin 15 between bobbins 9 and 10.

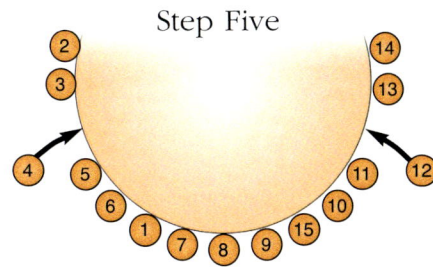

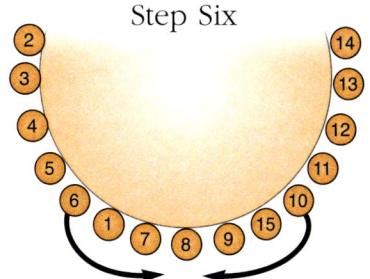

Step Five.
Move back towards the outer edges and drop bobbin 4 between 3 and 5, and drop bobbin 12 between 11 and 13.

Step Six.
Lift bobbins 6 and 10 and take them towards the centre going over two bobbins each.

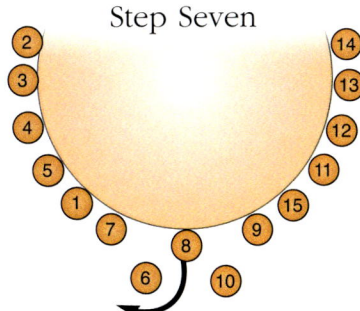

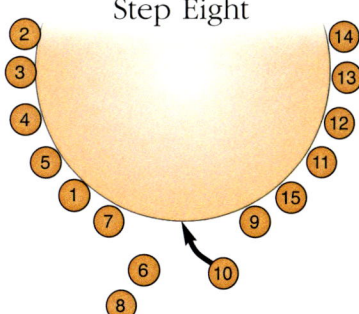

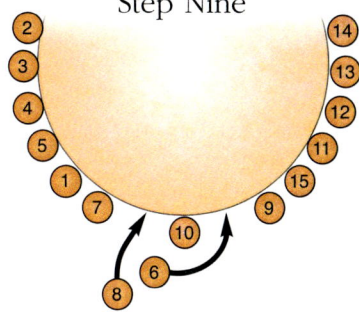

Step Seven.
Lift bobbin 8 onto the back of the left-hand thumb, above bobbin 6.

Step Eight.
Drop bobbin 10 at the centre of the stand.

Step Nine.
Drop bobbin 6 to the right of bobbin 10. Drop bobbin 8 to the left of bobbin 10.

Embroidery

Fig. 114.
Xiong Guiyang from Langde, Leishan County, Guizhou. She is stitching braid onto a sleeve panel that will be added to a festival jacket. The panel is made from layers of fabric and is firm enough to be worked unsupported. Work in progress is often kept clean with pieces of plastic bag that are temporarily stitched over the finished embroidery.

Embroidery

Introduction.

China has a reputation for producing fine embroidery. The neat and detailed work produced with a needle and thread is astounding. Yet the stitching required for braid embroidery is not as exacting. The stitches are functional, rather than decorative, with precision and conformity rarely being observed. This hardly detracts from the visual appearance, as the stitches are barely discernible amongst the braids. Today, the securing stitches vary considerably, not just from textile to textile, but also within the same piece. The stitching appears to be more a case of 'whatever is necessary,' rather than a set procedure. Because of this, the instructions given in this book are a selection out of the many options that have been studied.

Braid embroidery is used to decorate the surface of the fabric, although Fig. 115 shows a rare example of a braid actually being stitched back and forth through the fabric. The braids are attached in a variety of different ways, forming both flat and 3-dimensional decoration. Braid embroidery is usually accompanied by other decorative details, such as embroidery, fabric appliqué and other applied accessories.

The stitching is usually done in a 2-ply silk, though it is seldom the same shade as the braid. The Miao employ a useful technique that prevents the needle from slipping off the silk. The needle is threaded, then taken through the silk thread, as shown in Fig. 116. The start of the silk is knotted so that it will secure into the fabric. It is not uncommon to find that the other end is also knotted when the stitching has been completed. The braids are applied onto a fabric base, which is made from several layers of material. The firmness of the fabric layers means that embroidery frames are not required. Both ends of the braids are usually hidden. There are various ways in which this is done, such as tucking the ends back under themselves. The ends can also be hidden into the seam of the garment, or under other

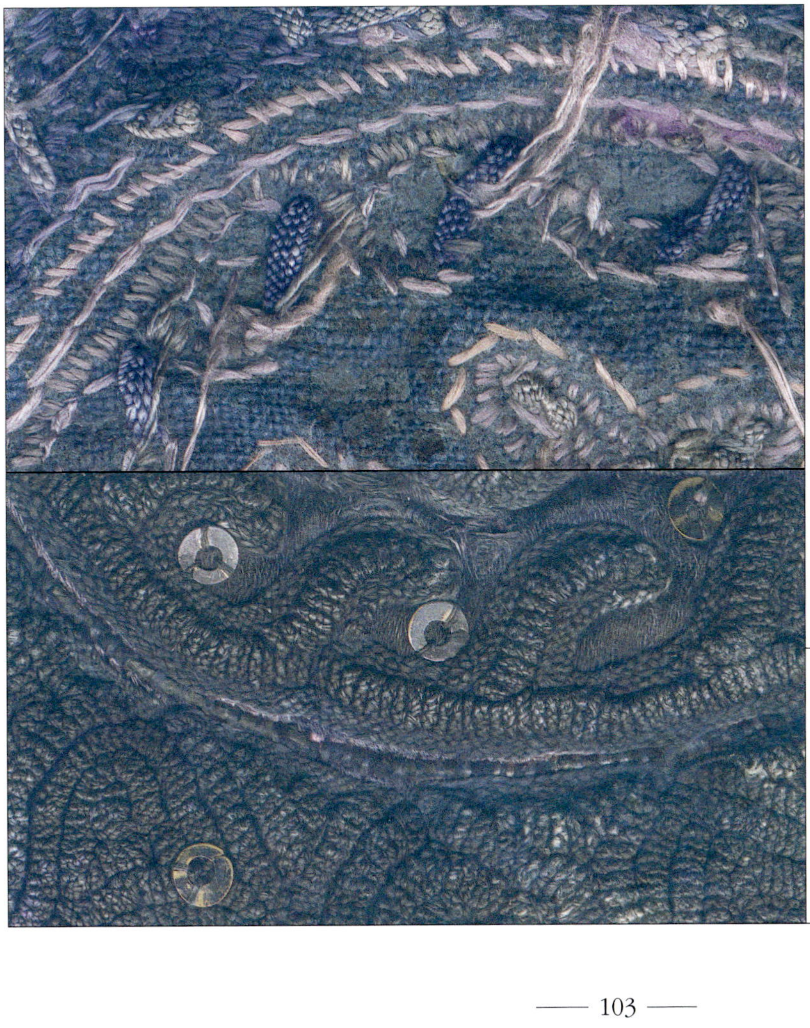

Fig. 115.
The back and front of an old Miao sleeve panel that has been overdyed in indigo. It shows a braid that is repeatedly drawn through the fabric. On the front, the braid is pleated to fill small dragon spines. The back shows where the braid has been stitched through the fabric along to the next scale motif.

Embroidery

applied pieces on the surface. On the more meticulous textiles, the braid ends are pulled to the back of the fabric (see Fig. 117).

It is possible to use any braid for the appliqué techniques. However, for aesthetic reasons, there is a tendency for certain braids to be selected for certain circumstances. The choice of braid is also influenced by the area and group to which the maker belongs. The fancy-patterned braids are most effective when they are lying flat, whilst plain braids are usually used for the more complex 3-dimensional work. The striped design is the exception, as this is particularly effective for all types of applied work.

The following chapter details some of the ways in which braids are applied onto fabric, with options on where to place the stitches. The diagrams illustrate the view from above the fabric's surface, with the black dots representing where the stitch enters, or exits, the fabric. The black line represents the stitches that show on the surface, whilst the dark red colour shows the path of the thread below the surface. The braid is shown as a pale ochre. For ease of identification, the outer edges of the braid are highlighted in different colours. Dotted lines are used when this edge is hidden under the braid.

Fig. 116.
The thread can be secured into the eye of the needle by piercing the needle point through the end of the silk.

Fig. 117.
Normally the start and finish of a braid are hidden from view. On the more meticulous pieces the ends are taken to the back of the fabric panel, as can be seen on the back of this Miao panel.
Courtesy of Gina Corrigan.

Flat Straight Border

The easiest form of braid embroidery is to couch the braid down in a flat, straight line. This style of work is frequently used as a highlight to a border edge. The braids are usually stitched down with a form of 'running' stitch. However, the firmness of the fabric makes it difficult for the needle to be worked in the conventional 'sewing' method. The 'sewing' method is where the needle makes an action parallel to the fabric so that the needle passes through the fabric twice in one go, and remains on the top surface of the fabric. Instead the 'stab' method is used, with the needle working perpendicular to the surface so that it passes completely through, from one side of the fabric to the other. This means that each running stitch is made of two movements. First the needle is taken through the fabric, from the back to the front surface. The thread is fully drawn through before the needle is returned to the back of the fabric. Once more the thread is fully drawn through before starting the whole process again. The 'running' stitches are arranged so that a small stitch appears on the front, whilst a longer float is made at the back. The stitch on the surface is usually so small that it is barely visible, whilst the stitch at the back can be anything up to 2 cm in length, though 5 to 7 mm is more usual. The haphazard nature of some of the work means that the running stitches are rarely straight or even. Occasionally, the stitches on the surface run parallel to the braid edge, but more often they are at a casual slant, some even sit perpendicular to the braid edge, or double back on themselves.

It is surprising how little stitching is required to keep a braid in place. Occasionally, more elaborate and secure stitching is used, though this tends to be for the wider braids. This can take the form of a row of zigzag stitches (see Fig. 118b), or a row of running stitch down each edge of the braid. Sometimes stitches are taken over the edge of the braid, though this is usually used when braids are sitting parallel to each other. Here, the stitch goes over the edge and into the adjacent braid so that both braid edges are secured in one go (see Fig. 118c). Sometimes the edge of the braid is deliberately caught by stitching that is being used to hold down other accessories, such as ribbon or cord. Fig. 111. shows an unusual example of blanket stitch making a more decorative method of attachment.

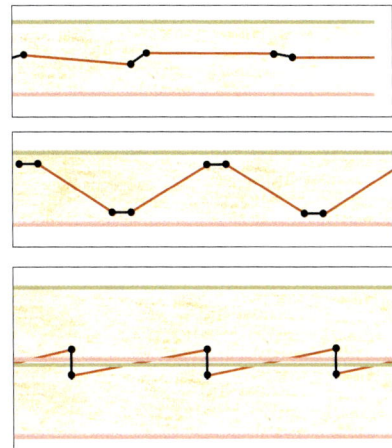

Fig. 118a (top).
Diagram showing the typical haphazard path of "running" stitch, with small stitches showing on the surface and longer floats at the back. This is the most common way in which individual braids are couched onto the fabric.

Fig. 118b (centre).
Diagram of the zigzag stitch that is sometimes used to secure wider braids.

Fig. 118c (bottom).
Diagram showing stitches made over the edge of a braid. These are often used to simultaneously attach adjacent braids.

Fig. 119.
The front and back of a Miao panel showing one of the neater examples of running stitch. The surface stitches are so small that the pink silk can barely be seen.

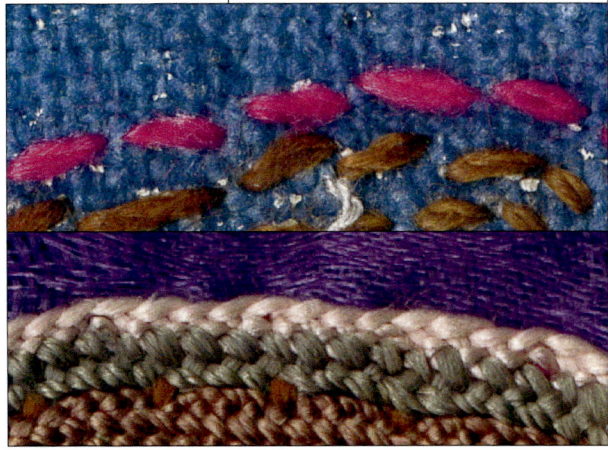

Curves & Corners

Braids are also applied onto the fabric surface in a flat but meandering line. The braid can be bent around a curve, or corner, in different ways. Here, they have been categorised into five different types: eased, puckered, tucked, coiled and folded. These corners and curves can be worked either clockwise or anticlockwise. The borders around the edge of a panel are usually worked anticlockwise, but the borders of interior motifs tend to be more adaptable. For convenience sake the diagrams are all shown working in an anti-clockwise direction.

Eased.

The unique nature of a braid's construction means that it can be eased around a tight corner, with individual parts of the structure contracting or expanding to fill the curve. The braid can remain flat depending on the type of braid, its tension and the angle of the turn. Stitching braids down in this manner is merely a case of continuing one of the methods used for applying flat, straight braids, except the braid is allowed to bend. Examples have been found where a stitch is placed at the mid-point of the turn, others have a stitch either side, whilst some appear quite arbitrary. Applying a small amount of pressure with the thumb on the turn point can help the braid to remain flat as it is eased around the corner.

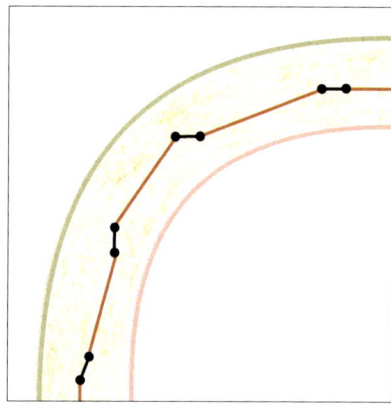

Puckered.

The point at which an eased braid no longer remains flat is the point at which a pucker is made. These can just be a natural consequence of the braid's limitation, or it can be made as a deliberate feature. A braid puckers when the contracting, inner edge of the curve, lifts, whilst the expanding, outer edge remains flat. This creates a small 3-dimensional bump, or angled ridge. Additional stitches are sometimes used to ensure that this pucker remains raised up from the fabric. These can be as straightforward as placing two 'running' stitches close together, one on either side of the pucker. A more distinctive version is to make an extra stitch, pinching the inner edges of the braid together, like a clasp at the base of a hood (see Fig 121). This option is sometimes accompanied by an extra stitch that secures the outer edge of the corner down against the fabric.

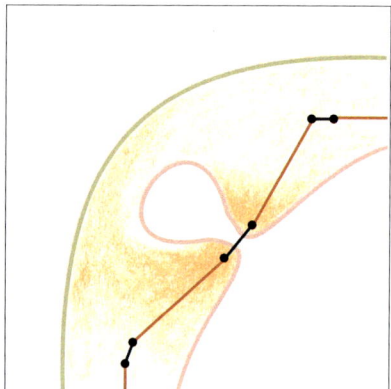

Embroidery

Tucked.

This type of corner is a deliberate way of keeping the braid flat, with the same face of the braid remaining upwards. The edge of the braid on the outer side makes a sharp turn, whilst the inner edge tucks under, doubling back on itself to take up the slack of the braid. This produces a right-angled corner with a mitred appearance. At minimum, a single stitch holds the tuck in place, through there are many other variations, such as a stitch over each edge of the braid, at the inner and outer corners. Use the needle, or thumbnail to help tuck in the inner part of the corner.

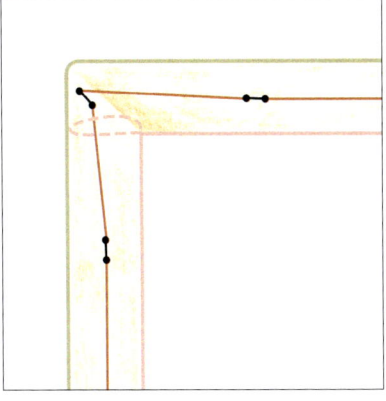

Coiled.

Here the braid is coiled around and then laid flat on the fabric's surface. This keeps the same face of the braid remaining upwards. This method can produce a slightly pointed corner, or a fuller angle depending on the position of the coil. A single stitch is usually sufficient to hold the coil in place, though the placement of this stitch varies. Many of these options pierce the coil, but Fig 123. shows one that takes the stitch through the coil. Other options, such as a two-stitch version, are also found. If the corner is to turn anticlockwise, then twist the braid to the right in a clockwise direction, and vice versa.

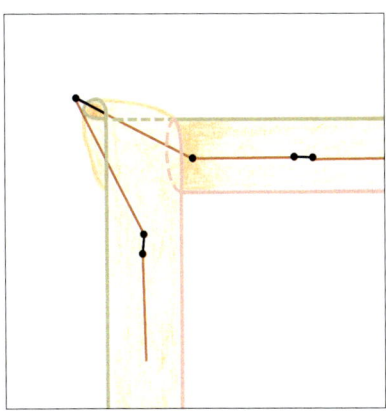

Folded.

Folding a corner causes the opposite surface of the braid to face upwards. The inner edge of the corner forms a sharp right-angled turn, whilst the outer corner is truncated so that two wider points are created. This type of corner is not often used on the patterned braids as the design can be disrupted when the braid is reversed. However, it is not noticed on the monotone braids, and some of the simpler patterns, such as the spot braid seen in Fig. 124. To make this corner, just flip the braid over so that the back surface is facing upwards and continue stitching down the braid.

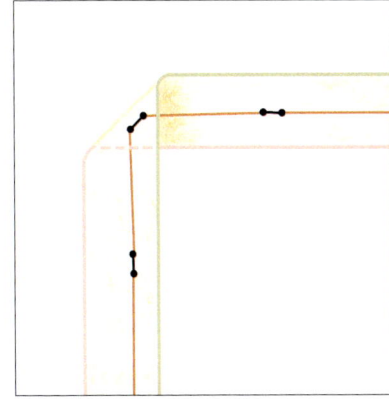

Embroidery

Types of Curves & Corners
(left to right from top).

Fig. 120.
Eased - The braids on this panel have turned sharp right-angled corners, yet they remain flat on the surface. The structure of the braid distorts to accommodate the angle.

Fig. 121.
Puckered - The inner edge of this braid has risen up off the surface of the fabric. It is held in place with an extra stitch which acts like the tie on a hood, drawing the base of the opening together.

Fig. 122.
Tucked - The outer edge of the braid remains flat on the surface whilst the inner edge is tucked under to take up the slack. This anticlockwise example is held in place with a single stitch over the fold line.

Fig. 123.
Coiled - The braid has been coiled around the needle then flattened against the fabric surface. This detail shows both a clockwise and anticlockwise coil. They are held in place with a single stitch that does not pierce the braid but sits inside the coil.

Fig. 124.
Folded - This corner has been worked clockwise. The braid has been folded over so that the opposite surface is facing upward. The visual appearance is not disrupted as the spot pattern looks similar on both sides.

Embroidery

The following 'in-action' photographs have been exaggerated in places in order to emphasis the technique. They illustrate one way of making puckered, tucked and coiled corners.

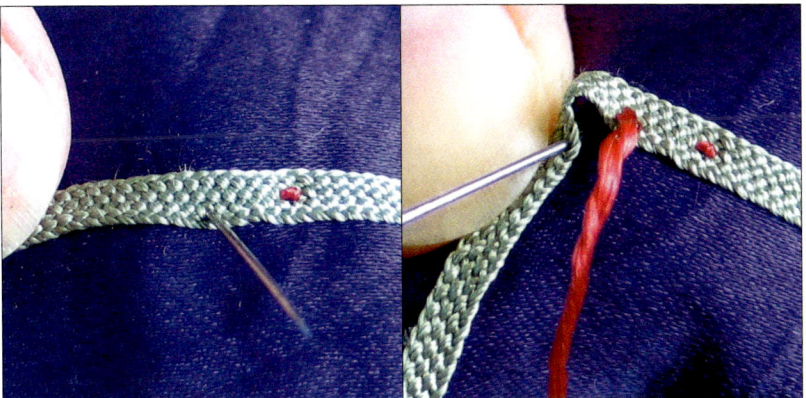

Fig. 125a & 125b.
Puckered Corner - Bring the tip of the needle to the front of the fabric, and out through the braid close to the inner edge where you want the braid to bend. Ease the braid round, keeping the outer edge of the braid flat against the fabric, but allow the inner edge to pucker up away from the surface. Bring the needle out of the fabric, and over the edge of the braid. Take it back into the edge of the braid on the other side of the pucker and down to the back of the fabric.

Fig 126.
Tucked Corner - Hold the braid down at the corner by laying the needle across the braid, perpendicular to the edges. Make the tuck by pushing the end of the braid over the needle with your thumb. Hold the corner down whilst it you remove the needle and stitch the braid into place.

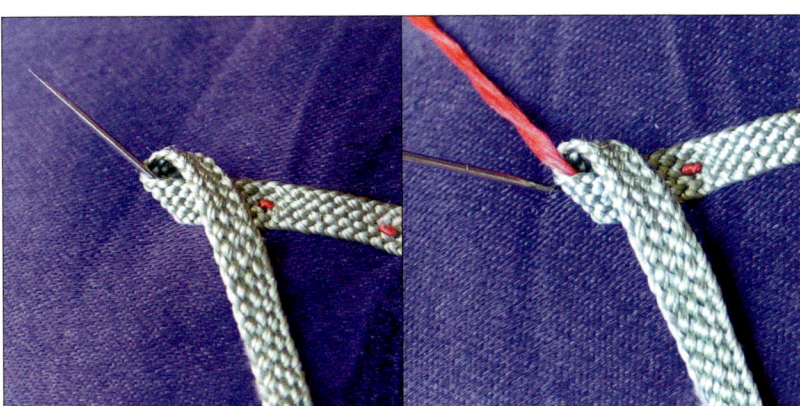

Fig. 127a & 127b.
Coiled Corner - Bring the tip of the needle out of the fabric and coil the braid around it in a clockwise direction. Draw the needle out through the fabric, and out through the top of the coil. Then take it back into the fabric over the edge of the braid, at the tip of the coil.

Regular Repeats

Curves and corners can be made at any point in the decorative work, whenever the braid needs to change direction. They can be used in several ways to create different effects. They may simply follow the contours of the textile's edge (such as seen in Fig. 129). Alternatively, the curves can be placed at regular repeated intervals to create specific patterns on the fabric. The following section details just six examples.

'Figure of Eight' Design.

This repeated 'figure-of-eight' motif is made from two braids that are eased into symmetric curves. Both braids repeatedly make opposite curves, intersecting one-another as they undulate along the edge. The crossover is alternated, with each braid taking a turn at going under or over. Because of this, both braids need to be stitched down at the same time. As this example is only 5 mm wide, a single row of stitching is sufficient. Here, just three stitches are made for each repeat; once at the peak of each curve and another at the overlap of the braids (as shown in the diagram).

The diagram (above) shows the path of the stitches couching down the 'figure-of-eight' braids in Fig. 128.

Fig. 128.
This Bouyei girl's jacket has a 'figure-of-eight' design running along the base edge. The braids are the same structure as JC1, and are less than 2 mm wide. *Courtesy of Martin Conlan.*

Embroidery

'Fret' Design.

A single braid is eased around the contours of this design. Four right-hand turns are followed by four left-hand turns, and so the pattern continues.

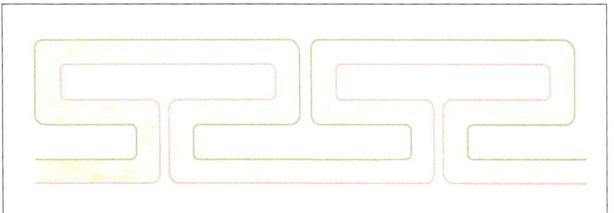

Fig. 129.
Nine different braid structures are used for the applied decoration on this baby's bib. The close-up shows a green and white version of braid JC4 that has been eased around to form the geometric 'fret' design.

Embroidery

'Looped' Border Design.

Looped borders make an attractive change to straightedged ones. The braid can be eased into a complete loop at regular intervals. The example shown in Fig. 130 is a two-braid version. The pink and white striped braid is stitched down and eased into a coil every 2 to 3 cm. A second, orange and green braid is added above the first. It has been eased around the loops of the first braid and makes its own loop between each of the pink and white ones. The white stitching on this particular example is rather clumsy and much of the stitching shows on the surface. A single braid 'looped' border can be seen in Fig. 80.

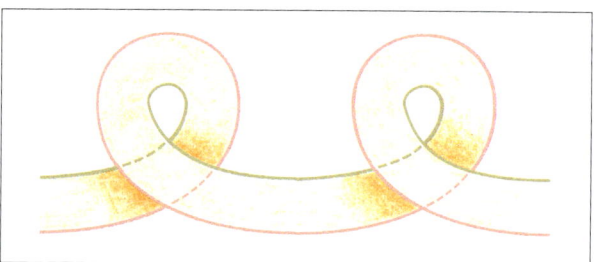

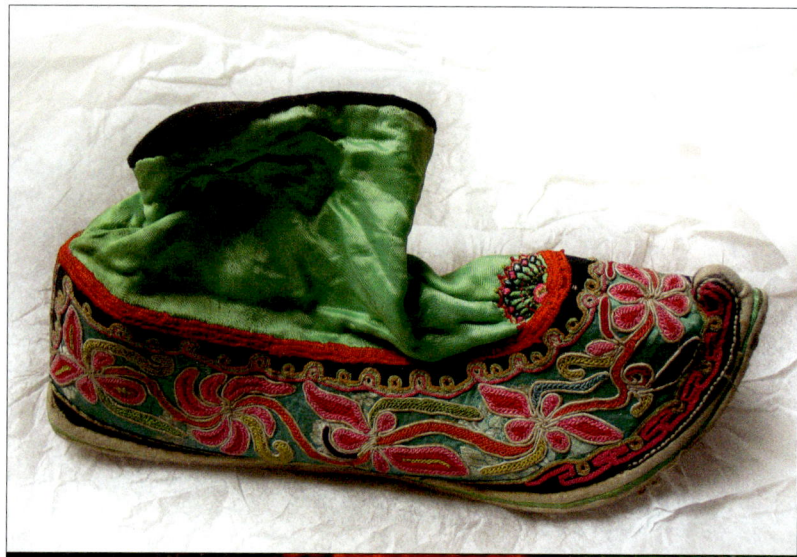

Fig. 130.
A 'looped' border design found on a pair of shoes. This version is made using two different striped braids, both of which are braid structure JC4. They have been eased into loops and stitched down with white silk.
Courtesy of Gina Corrigan.

Embroidery

'Scalloped' Design.

A scalloped line employs two types of curves working alternately, usually an eased and a puckered curve. They can be used as an independent feature, but they are usually found forming a border to a motif. In these circumstances, the rounded edges are normally made with the puckered curve closest to the motif with the braid lifting away from the centre. This typical format is illustrated in Fig. 131. Here, the scallops curve tightly round to form the border of a small circular motif. Two different types of curve are used in Fig. 132. Here, an eased curve is followed by a coiled one.

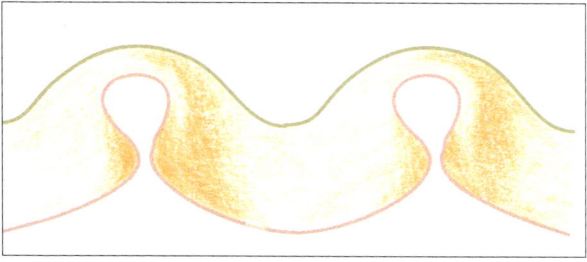

Fig. 131 (right).
Detail from the Miao jacket seen in Fig 91. The circular motif is bordered with a 'scalloped' edge made from two different types of curves. The curves furthest from the motif's centre are eased, whilst the inner curves are puckered up. The whole motif is less than 4 cm diameter.
Courtesy of Debbie James.

Fig. 132 (below).
Detail from the cuff of the Bouyei jacket shown in Fig. 128. A subtly different scallop effect is created when the curves are alternately eased-then-coiled, rather than eased-then-puckered.
Courtesy of Martin Conlan.

Embroidery

'Rounded Zigzag' Design.

This technique is often found shaping the little spines on Miao dragons. They are normally made from striped braids, which adds to the visual effect. Both turns of the zigzag are made with puckered corners which produces a 3-dimensional ribbed texture with smooth rounded edges. They tend to be stitched down with the overlapping stitches shown in Fig 118c, with extra stitches at the turns.

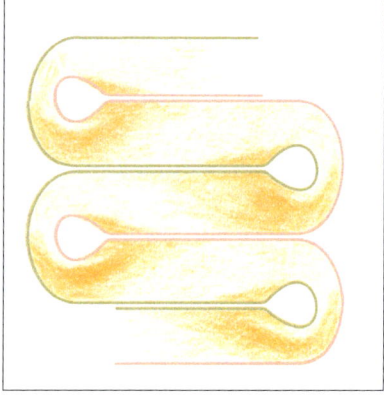

Fig. 133.
A two-coloured striped braid, JC4, makes a 'rounded zigzag' border. It forms the little spines on the dragon motif in Fig. 89. The braid makes a sharp turn with a puckered corner before doubling back on itself ready for the next turn.
Courtesy of Gina Corrigan.

Fig. 134.
Another version of the 'rounded zigzag' found on a Miao jacket from Taijiang County. Here, each circular motif is made from a braid eased into a small ring. The ring is then bordered by two rings of 'rounded zigzags'.

Embroidery

'Angular Zigzag' Design.

This zigzag feature is more angular than the previous one. This is caused by the nature of the turns. Here, coiled corners are used for each turn, though they must alternate between clockwise and anticlockwise twists. The example shown is made with a monotone braid and is worked so that a space is left between each turn.

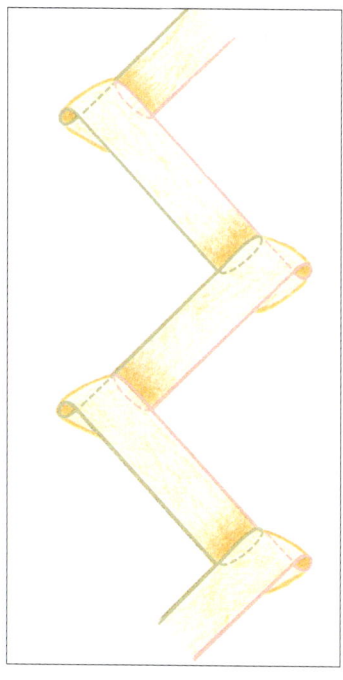

Fig. 135.
A sleeve panel from a Miao festival jacket. This 'angular zigzag' design is made with coiled corners. They must be worked with alternate left and right-hand turns as shown in diagram above.
Courtesy of Gina Corrigan.

Motifs

The majority of braids are couched down as a border, either defining the garment's edge or framing a detail of its decoration. However, braid embroidery can be very effective when it is used for creating motifs. This style of work is widely used by the Miao from the Leishan, Kaili and Taijiang counties of East Guizhou, though it is not exclusive to them. There are different methods of making braid motifs, and they vary in the amount of braid, and skill, required to produce them. The 3-dimensional versions are the more complex and braid consuming.

Outline.

This type of motif making is the simplest. Here, a braid is couched down so that it follows the contours of the motif. The corners and curves can be negotiated in any of the ways described earlier (see page 106). It is not uncommon to find a combination used in one piece, depending on the degree of the turn. The example shown in Fig. 136 uses a selection of eased and folded curves.

Fig. 136.
A blue and white version of braid JC6 has been eased and folded so that it creates the outline of a bat motif. The bat is a popular design in China as the word sounds the same as 'blessing'.

Embroidery

Flat Filling.

A solid motif can be made entirely from braids. The designs can be filled in with braids that are laid flat. The outline is worked first, often with a striped braid. When the border braid is in place, the interior area is filled in, starting with the outside edge and gradually working inward. A monotone braid is usually used for the filling. It is stitched down flat with eased, puckered or tucked curves and corners. Some stitchers deliberately aim to produce a more 3-dimensional look to the motifs, without using large quantities of braid. This can be achieved by emphasing the puckered corners using the stitch shown in Fig. 125. This enhances the puckers and produces a slightly knobbly texture such as can be seen in Fig. 138.

Fig. 137 (above and left).
Two square panels for Miao baby carriers, both at different stages of production. The outline braids are stitched down first, then the interior areas are filled with plain braids that are couched down flat.

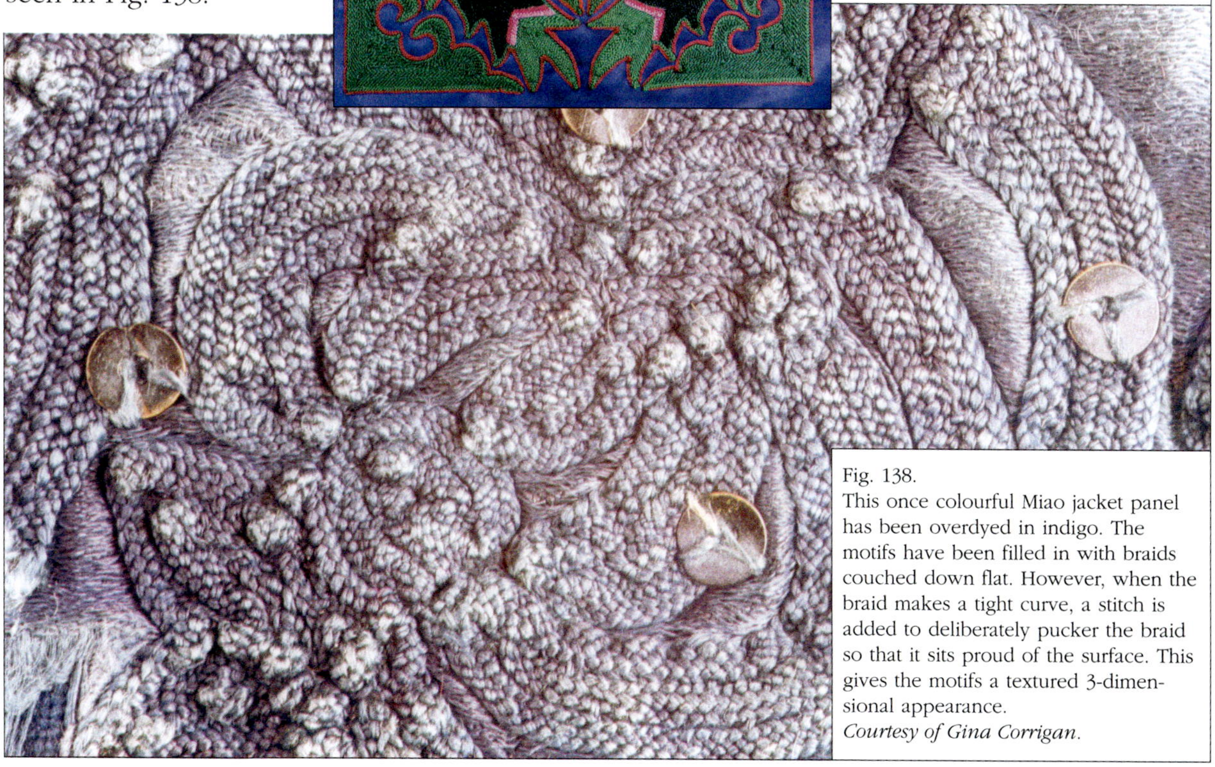

Fig. 138.
This once colourful Miao jacket panel has been overdyed in indigo. The motifs have been filled in with braids couched down flat. However, when the braid makes a tight curve, a stitch is added to deliberately pucker the braid so that it sits proud of the surface. This gives the motifs a textured 3-dimensional appearance.
Courtesy of Gina Corrigan.

Embroidery

Pleating.

Pleating is the simplest and most widely used of the 3-dimensional forms of braid embroidery. Pleated braids are used to make entire motifs, or to fill areas within a motif outlined with flat braid. As usual, there are different ways in which the pleating can be held in place. The stitches all sit perpendicular to the braid edges, holding the trough of the pleat against the fabric. The most secure version is made by piercing the braid on both its upward and downward journey (Fig. 139a). Alternative versions either pierce the braid just once, or straddle the braid completely (Fig. 139c). The pleats are often made with a monotone braid, though the structure varies. Striped patterns are not uncommon as they give an interesting decorative effect (see Fig. 140). The older, better

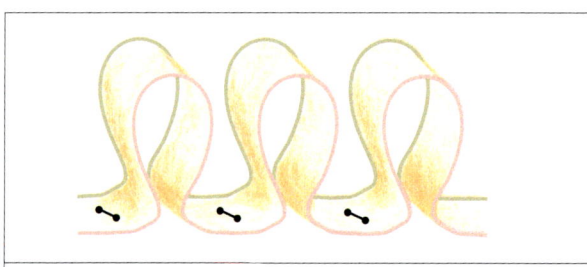

Diagram showing a stylised side view of the pleating.

quality handiwork has tightly packed pleats with anything over 10 pleats per cm, though today it is usually a lot looser. The pleats rise up from the fabric by about 1 to 2 mm, creating a rich sculptural effect. The even spacing of these pleats is helped by using the needle (see Fig. 142).

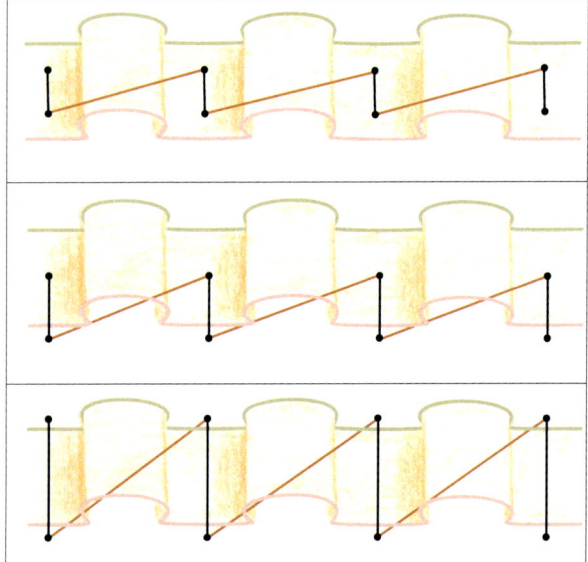

Different ways of stitching the pleating.
Fig. 139a (top).
Perpendicular stitches exit and enter the braid.
Fig. 139b (centre).
Perpendicular stitches exit the fabric beside the braid then enter the braid.
Fig. 139c (bottom).
Perpendicular stitches exit and enter the fabric either side of the braid.

Fig. 140.
Striped braids can be used to good effect when they are pleated. This detail is from the panel shown in Fig. 89.
Courtesy of Gina Corrigan.

Embroidery

Fig. 141.
Pleated braids give a rich textural filling to motifs. This example from Langde, Leishan County uses braid JC1, and is stitched down using the version shown in Fig. 139a.
Courtesy of Gina Corrigan.

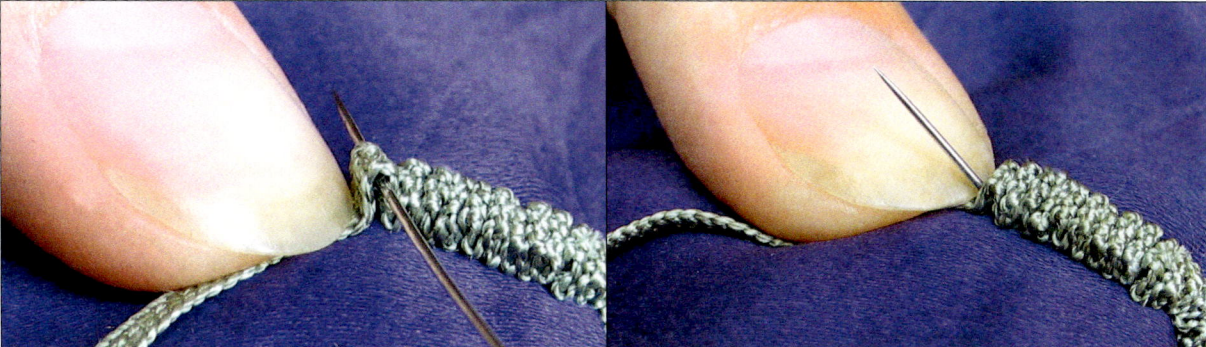

Fig. 142.
Use the needle to lift the braid up against the previous pleat (if you are using the stitching shown in Fig. 139a, then the needle needs to be brought to the surface, around the panel's edge). Push the braid up against the needle with your thumbnail and hold it down whilst you stitch this new pleat in place. Try to bring the needle up through the fabric and braid as close to the pleat as possible.

Embroidery

Coiling.

This is basically the same as a coiled corner, except that the coil is secured so that it remains upright on the surface of the fabric, forming a 3-dimensional cone shape. Unlike the coiled corner, the stitches sit at the base of the cone rather than flattening it against the fabric. As usual, there are themes and variations with the stitching, ranging from one to three stitches per coil. The three stitch version shown in Fig. 144 is found on the better quality work, as it holds the coiled conical shapes firmly in place. Photographs detailing the first stages of this method are shown in Fig. 146. The braid can be coiled to the left or right, though twisting the braid clockwise is the usual direction. Motifs can be filled in by stitching the coils close together. They can also be carefully placed to form regular designs like those shown in Fig. 145. Once again striped braids add a distinctive look to the coils, by giving them a contrasting tip. This effect can be created because one edge of the braid remains flat against the fabric, whilst the other edge rises and falls to form the conical tip.

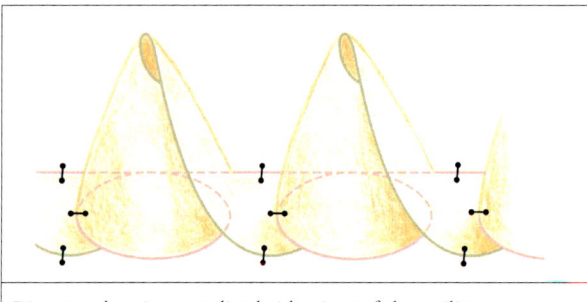

Diagram showing a stylised side view of the coiling.

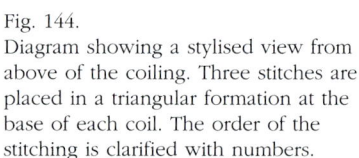

Fig. 144.
Diagram showing a stylised view from above of the coiling. Three stitches are placed in a triangular formation at the base of each coil. The order of the stitching is clarified with numbers.

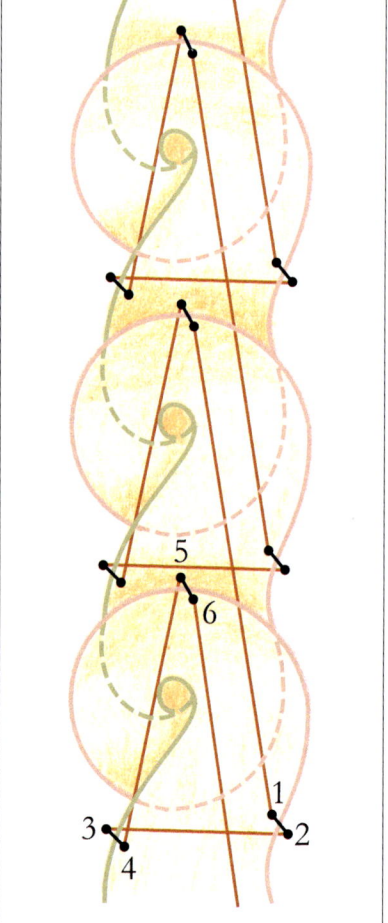

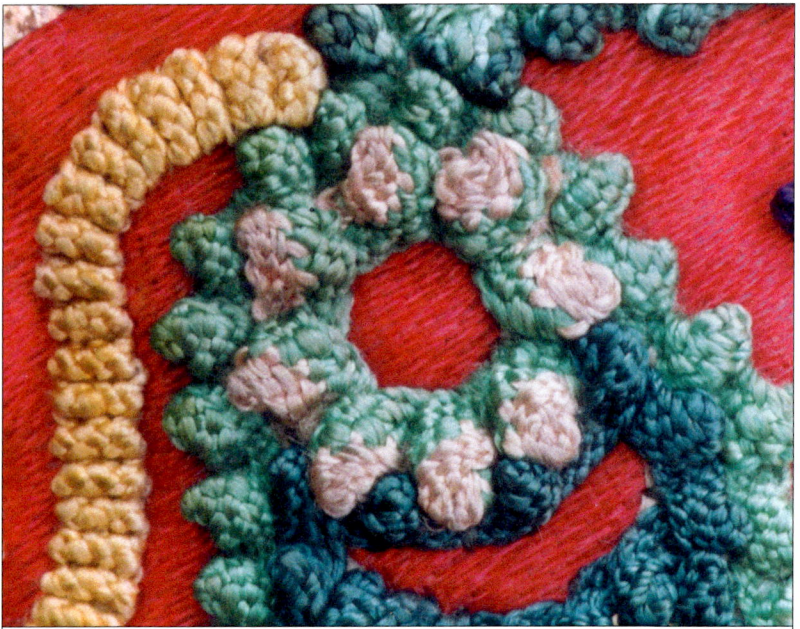

Fig. 143.
Detail from Miao panel with pleated and coiled braids. The green cones with peach tips are made by coiling a striped braid, which is similar in structure to braid JC14. The green edge of the braid stays close to the surface of the fabric, whilst the peach edge rises and falls to make the cones.
Courtesy of Ien Rappoldt.

Embroidery

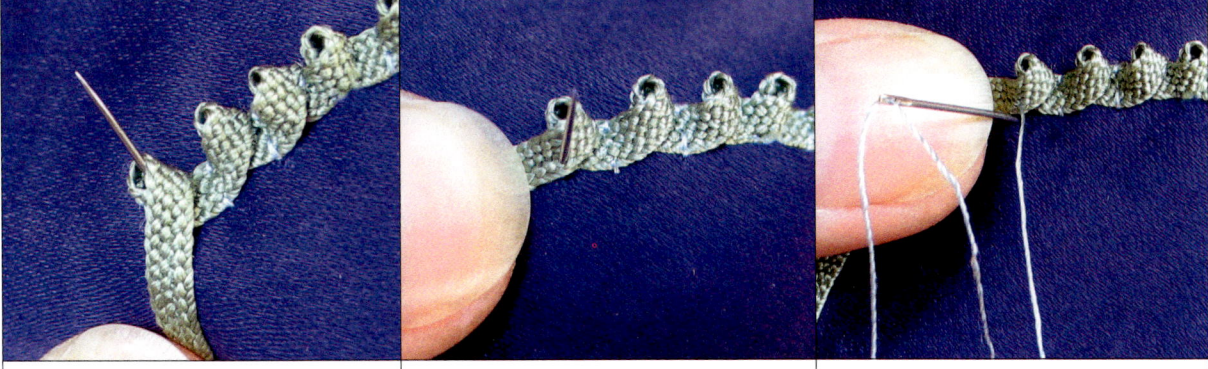

Fig. 145.
A Miao sleeve panel with motifs made from tightly packed coiled braids. The monotone, and striped-patterned braids are all twisted in a clockwise direction. They are secured with the three stitch method shown in Fig. 144. The work is very precise as can be seen in the detail (left) where each cone-shape is lined up to form a regular ridge at the centre of this dragon motif. The braid is a 2 mm wide version of JC1.

Fig. 146a.
Bring the tip of the needle out of the fabric to the lower right of where you wish to place the new coil (the point marked 1 in Fig. 144). Coil the braid around the needle in a clockwise direction, so that the coil sits upright like a cone on the fabric.

Fig. 146b.
Partially draw back the needle and bring the tip of the needle out through the braid at the lower right base of the coil (marked 1 in Fig. 144).

Fig. 146c.
Draw the needle out, then take it into the fabric at the edge of the braid (marked 2 in Fig. 144) One, or two, more stitches can now be added around the base of the coil. Fig. 144 shows the path taken when two more stitches are added.

Embroidery

Triangular Coiling.

This is another version of coiling, typically found on Dong textiles. Here, the nature of the braid plays an important part in creating the effect. The best results are achieved with a braid structure that has a high difference in ratio between its width and thinness. This type of structure helps to improve the appearance by folding into neat angular triangles that are not too bulky. Typically, a plain oblique interlaced braid, like JC14, is used. Ideally, the braid should be made with a firm tight tension, as this also helps to enhance the result.

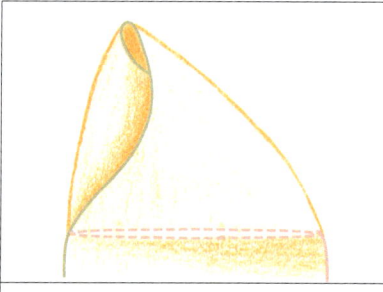

Diagram showing a stylised end view of the triangular coiling.

The triangular coiling is often used for making little silk 'dragons' (see Fig. 147). Here the braid is folded into a row of triangles that curve along one side of a spine feature. The row then turns and works its way down the other side. The coils are pushed into much more angular folds so that they form flat triangles, rather than circular cones. One edge of the triangle sits on the fabric whilst the other two sides

Fig. 147.
Detail showing the 3-dimensional nature of triangular coiling. The sinuous silk 'dragon' on this Dong panel is made from a braid coiled into a row of folded triangles.
Courtesy of Gina Corrigan.

Embroidery

rise up from the fabric. The sides of the triangle are not equal so their meeting point slopes off to one side, normally to the left as the preference is for clockwise twists. The better quality examples have tightly packed triangles with up to 10 per cm. Again there is a wide range of stitching methods used. The three-stitch version shown in Fig 144 can be used although the distance between the coils is decreased, and the angle of the coil is altered. Fig. 148 showns a two-stitch version that it also used.

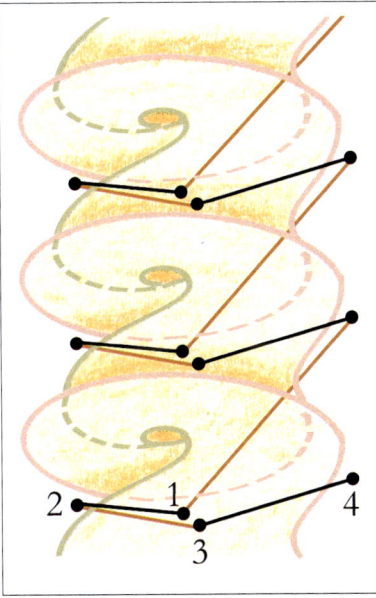

Fig. 148.
Diagram showing a stylised view from above the coiling. The numbers help to clarify the order of the stitching.

Fig. 149.
This detail from a Dong panel shows another use of triangular coiling. Here, the row of coiling is worked into a circle, with the raised triangles sloping outwards to create a bowl shape. A padded fabric ball sits inside the hollow, which is just 1.5 cm wide.
Courtesy of Ien Rappoldt.

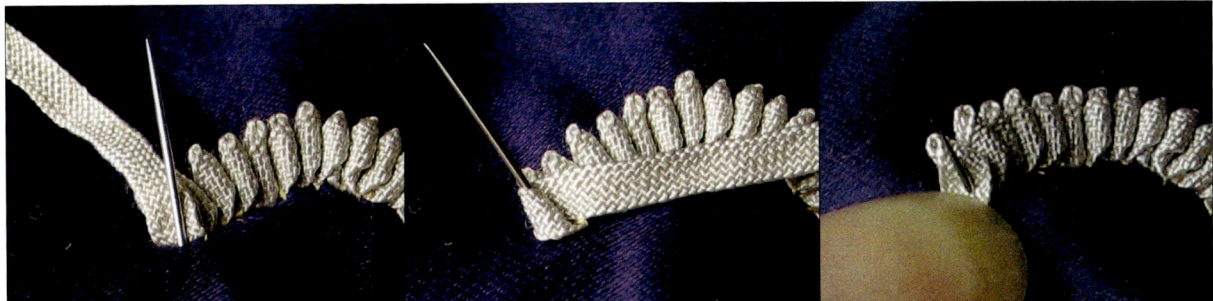

Fig. 150a.
Bring the tip of the needle out of the fabric, close to the previous coil (the point marked 1 in Fig. 148).

Fig. 150b.
Coil the braid clockwise around the needle so that is forms a folded triangular shape rather than a circular coil. One side of the triangle lies flat across the surface of the fabric. The other two rise up, with one of them angling up to the left.

Fig. 150c.
Bring the braid to the front of the coil and lay it flat against the surface of the fabric. Use your thumbnail to push the coil close up against the previous one. Draw back the needle and insert it through the braid, in front of the coil (marked as 1 in Fig. 148). Add the two stitches shown in Fig. 148 to secure the coil in place.

Embroidery

Overlaid Loops.

This is a rarer type of braid embroidery, found on the better quality Miao textiles. It is usually used to shape part of a dragon's body. The scalelike texture is created from loops of braid that have been puckered to form raised dimples. The loops are staggered so that they overlap one another. As the overlaid curve of the loop is puckered in the opposite direction to that of the curve underneath it, the whole feature rises up into firm peaks. It is typically made with a wide striped braid such as JC13. The stitching is worked where necessary to hold the edges of the braid in place. The path of the stitching becomes quite complex as the loops and stitching overlap (see Fig. 155).

Fig. 151.
Detail from an old Miao panel from Taijiang County. This one has been overdyed in indigo, emphasising the textural nature of the appliqué. The overlaid coils forming the dragon's body are made from braid JC13 and would once have been two different colours.
Courtesy of Gina Corrigan.

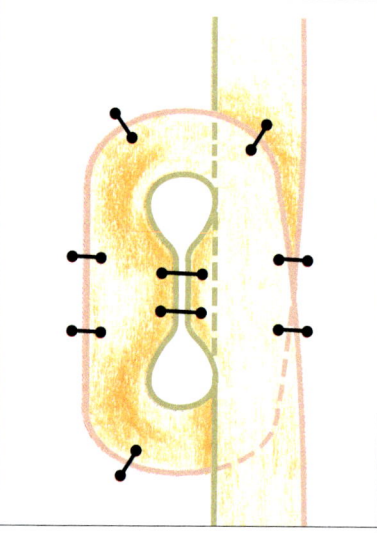

Fig. 152.
Diagrams showing the stylised view from above. Each loop is made from two tight puckered curves. The loops overlap each other to form the raised feature.

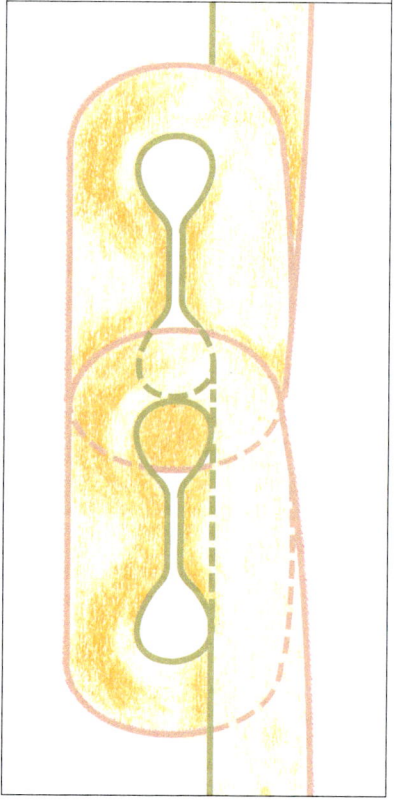

Embroidery

Fig. 153a.
The new loop starts as the old one ends. Stitch down the braid on the right-hand side.

Fig. 153b.
Just below the old loop, double back the braid to form a tight puckered corner. Stitch the pucker and left edge.

Fig. 153c.
As the new loop starts to overlap the old one, double back the braid forming a tight pucker over the top of the previous one. Stitch in place.

Fig. 154.
Detail from the old Miao panel shown on the front cover. The main body of the dragon motif is built up from overlaid loops.
Courtesy of Gina Corrigan.

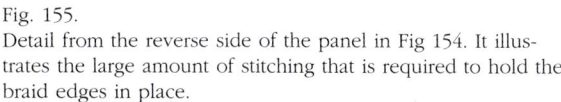

Fig. 155.
Detail from the reverse side of the panel in Fig 154. It illustrates the large amount of stitching that is required to hold the braid edges in place.
Courtesy of Gina Corrigan.

Notes

1. The terms 'embroidery' and 'appliqué' have both been used to describe the applying of braids onto fabric to form decorative features. Although the stitching is subordinate to the braid, the decision was made to use the older of the two definitions as a preference.

2. Metric measurements are used throughout this book. An approximate conversion into imperial is as follows: 1 mm = 0.039 inches, 1 cm = 0.39 inches, 1 gm =0.035 ounces.

3. This book refers to braid 'structure' as the physical interlacing of the strands, whilst the braid 'pattern' is a visual effect caused by the arrangement of colour on the structure. For example, Braid JC1, JC2 and JC3 are different patterns created on the same braid structure.

4. The Chinese people consist of 56 officially recognised ethnic groups. The Han Chinese are the largest group, making up over 90% of the population. The Miao, known as the Hmong outside of China, are one of the many minority groups.

5. Of course, there could be much that has yet to be recorded, but the trend appears to be heading towards this gradual loss of skill.

6. Such as the two-layered braid with animal motifs excavated from Yingpan, Xinjiang (Zhao 1999:86)

7. This could be caused by a bias in the collected items - a more thorough survey would be needed before this could be confirmed

8. British Museum accession number 1895-189.

9. For example, although many Miao are unaware of the technique, Ien Rappoldt has observed a group from Rongjiang county, in Guizhou, using this method.

10. The Mien are a subgroup of the Yao. They originated in China and have migrated south into bordering countries, such as Laos.

11. Personal communication with Ny Ting, a Lao Mien braidmaker.

12. A few braids display characteristics that are indicative of neither the loop-manipulation, nor the stand & bobbin method. This suggests the possibility of a third, as yet unknown, technique.

13. For example, the loop-manipulated insert on the Uppsala Sudary (Speiser 1997).

14. For example, the sample in Lady Bindloss's 17th century instruction book (Carey 2003:35).

15. For example, by the 18th century Diderot (1751) makes a clear distinction between the two techniques.

16. Missionaries have been responsible for introducing other ideas, for example they introduced potato growing to the Miao in southeast Guizhou (de Beauclair 1960:146).

17. For example, convents in Valenciennes, France, provided the training and employment for the majority of the lacemakers producing this renowned bobbin lace (Malotet 1927)

18. Braids made from metallic threads are found on items throughout Asia and Europe, and they could share a common heritage. They have been found on Chinese objects (such as the Manchu cuffs in Fig. 8) but they are not detailed in this book, although they do share some similarities to the type illustrated.

19. Shed is a weaving term used to describe the space created between warp threads. It is formed by lifting, or depressing, some of the threads, and allows the weft to pass easily through the space from one edge of the warp to the other.

20. The Dong people are another of China's minority groups.

21. The Miao minority group live in southern China, and down into the bordering countries. Outside of China they refer to themselves as Hmong as they feel that Miao is a derogatory term.

22. These were collected by Augustine Henry prior to 1898. They are now part of the collection held at the Whitworth Art Gallery, Manchester.

23. Until a form of romanised script was introduce in the 1950's.

24. Boudet (2002) offers an interpretation of some of the designs meaning.

25. The flat surface is not entirely redundant as it can be used whilst braiding is in progress. For example, Mrs Xiong (Fig. 28) uses it to rest her glasses on.

26. A Chinese minority group.

Bibliography

ADSHEAD, S. 1997. Material Culture in Europe and China 1400-1800. Basingstoke: Macmillan Press Ltd.
BABER, E. 1882. Travels and Researches in Western China. London: John Murray.
BEAUCLAIR, I. 1970. A Miao Tribe of Southeast Kweichow and its Cultural Configuration. In Tribal Cultures of Southwest China. Taipei: The Orient Cultural Service, 60-145.
BERLINER, N. 1986. Chinese Folk Art. New York: Little Brown & Co
BOUDOT, E. 2002. Motifs plus récents inspirés de la culture Han. In: Costumes Traditionnels de la Chine. Lyon: Musée des Tissus. 20-43.
BUXTON, D. 1929. China - the Land and the People. Oxford: Clarendon Press.
CAREY, J. 2003. Braids and Beyond - a Broad Look at Narrow Wares. Ottery St Mary: Carey Company.
CATLIN, A. 1987. Textiles as Texts - Arts of Hmong Women from Laos. Los Angeles: The Woman's Building.
CHABROS, K. & BATCULUUN, L. 1993. Mongol Examples of Proto-Weaving. Central Asiatic Journal 37 (1-2), 20-32.
CHINA HOUSE GALLERY.1988. Richly Woven Traditions - Costumes of the Miao of Southwest China and Beyond. New York: China House Gallery.
CLARKE, S. 1911. Among the Tribes in Southwest China. London: Morgan and Scott.
CORRIGAN, G. 2001. Miao textiles from China. London: British Musuem Press.
DIDEROT, D. 1751. Encyclopedie ou Dictionnaire raisonne des Sciences, des Arts et des Metiers. Paris.
DOOLITTLE, J. 1865. Social Life of the Chinese. New York: Harper and Brothers.
FRASER, L. 2004. A Language of Textiles: Exploration of a Miao Jacket from Southwest China. Textile, 2(1), 46-51.
GARRETT, V. 1989. Traditional Chinese Clothing in Hong Kong and South China 1840-1980. Oxford: Oxford University Press.
GOLDMAN, A. 1995. Lao Mien Embroidery. Bangkok: White Lotus.
HAIG, P. & SHELTON, M. 2006. Threads of Gold. Chinese Textiles: Ming to Ch'ing. Atglen: Schiffer.
HANYU, G. 1992. Chinese Textile Design. London: Penguin Books.
HOMMEL, R. 1969.(1937) China at work : an illustrated record of the primitive industries of China's masses, whose life is toil, and thus an account of Chinese civilization. London: MIT Press
JACKSON, A. & JAFFER, A. (eds). 2004. Encouters: The Meeting of Asia and Europe 1500-1800. London: V&A Publications
JACKSON, B. 1997. Splendid Slippers. Berkeley: Ten Speed Press.
KINOSHITA, M. 1994. Study of Archaic Braiding Techniques in Japan. Kyoto: Kyoto Shoin.
KO, D. 2001. Every Step a Lotus: Shoes for Bound Feet. Berkeley:University of California Press
LAUMANN, M. 1993. Miao Textile Design. Taipei: Fu Jen Catholic University Press.
LEONG, Y & TAO, L. 1915. Village and Town Life in China. London: George Allen & Unwin Ltd.
LEVEY, S. 1983. Lace: A History. London: V&A Publications.
MALOTET, A. 1927. La Dentelle a Valenciennes. Paris: Jean Schemit.
McDANIEL, P. & GARDINER, L. 2002. Silver and Silk. San Diego: Mingei International Museum.
MINICK, S. & PING, J. 1996. Arts and Crafts of China. London: Thames & Hudson.
NEEDHAM, J. 1985. Science and Civilisation in China. Cambridge: Cambridge University Press.
O'CONNOR, D. 1994a. Best bib and tucker: Embroidery on Miao jackets from Guizhou province. Embroidery. 45(3),152-4.
O'CONNOR, D. 1994b. Miao Costumes. Farnham: James Hockey Gallery.
ORIENTATIONS. 1998. Chinese and Central Asian Textiles. Selected articles from Orientations 1983-1997 Hong Kong: Orientations Magazine Ltd
POPOV, A. 1955. Pletenie i tkacestvo u narodov Sibiri v XIX i pervoi cetverti XX stoletiya. Sbornik Muzeya Antropologii i Etnografii XVI 41-146.
RAPPOLDT, I. 2005. Geweven Verhalen. Abcoude: Uniepers.
ROSSI, G. 1987. A Flourishing Art: China. Threads 9, 30-32.
SMITH, A. 1894. Chinese Characteristics. New York: Fleming Revell Company.

SMITH, R. 2005. Miao Embroidery from South West China. Bognor Regis: Occidor Ltd.
SPEISER, N. 1997. A Loop-braided Lace Insertion on a Late Medieval Sudary in Uppsala Cathedral. Cieta Bulletin 74, 96-107.
START, L. & WRIGHT, M. 1936. Decorated Textiles from Yunnan Collected by Augustine Henry, 1896-1898. The Manchester Memoirs. 80(8), 59-84.
STEIN, A. 1921. Serindia: Detailed Report of Explorations in Central Asia and Westernmost China. Oxford: Clarendon.
TORIMARU, S. 2001. Spiritual Fabric. Fukuoka: Akishige Tada.
VAINKER, S. 2004. Chinese Silk - a Cultural History. London: British Museum Press.
VOLLER, J. 1980. Five Colours of the Universe. Alberta: Edmorton Art Gallery.
VOLLER, J. 1999. Chinese Costume and Accessories 17th-20th Century. Paris: AEDTA.
WATT, J. & WARDWELL, A. 1997. When Silk was Gold. New York: Metropolitan Musuem of Art.
WELLS, P. & HILL, L. 1991. Costumes and Embroideries of the Ethnic Minorities of S.W. China. Hull: Centre for S.E. Asian Studies, University of Hull.
WHITFIELD, S. (ed). 2004. The Silk Road. London: British Library.
WILSON, V. 1986. Chinese Dress. London: Victoria & Albert Museum.
WILSON, V. 2005. Chinese Textiles. London: Victoria & Albert Museum.
ZHAO, F. 1999. Treasures in Silk. Hong Kong: Costume Squad Ltd.

Details about equipment and other books by
Jacqui Carey can be found by contacting

Carey Company

Summercourt
Ridgeway
Ottery St Mary
Devon
EX11 1DT
England
Tel/Fax: (0) 1404 813486
e-mail: carey@careycompany.com
www.careycompany.com